Potential

.

—

Potential

Workplace Violence Prevention
and Your Organizational Success

Bill Whitmore

Chairman & CEO, AlliedBarton Security Services

HIGHPOINT
EXECUTIVE PUBLISHING
www.highpointpubs.com

New York — Los Angeles

This edition published by HIGHPOINT EXECUTIVE PUBLISHING.

For information, write to info@highpointpubs.com.

First Edition

ISBN: 978-0-98394-320-4

Library of Congress Cataloging-in-Publication Data

Whitmore, Bill

POTENTIAL: Workplace Violence Prevention and Your Organizational Success, 1st Edition

Includes index.

Summary: "AlliedBarton Security Services CEO Bill Whitmore explains what organizations of all sizes can do to prevent workplace violence from occurring, while at the same time enhancing overall morale, health and profitability."—Provided by publisher.

ISBN: 978-0-98394-320-4 (hardbound)

1.Business 2.Management 3. Industrial Health and Safety

Library of Congress Control Number: 2011936855

Design by Sarah M. Clarehart

Manufactured in the United States of America

10 9 8 7 6 5 4 3 2 1

Contents

CHAPTER 3: Embracing the Cold Hard Truth

CHAPTER 4: Establishing Next Practices for Your Organization

PART TWO: ENABLING YOUR SECURE ORGANIZATION
CHAPTER 5: Creating Security with Leadership

CHAPTER 6: Nurture Employee Engagement

CHAPTER 7: Encourage Individual Growth

CHAPTER 10: Securing Healthcare

CHAPTER 11: Looking Ahead to a Secure, Profitable Future

Foreword

by Michael McCann, former United Nations Security Chief and President of McCann Protective Services

An innovative security veteran, Bill Whitmore has long been widely recognized as one of the nation's most dynamic and knowledgeable experts in physical security, a vital industry that has gained a greater level of importance and interest since the bombing of the Oklahoma City Alfred P. Murrah Federal Building in 1995 and the 9/11 terrorist attacks in New York and Washington. His vast experience and knowledge span both the private and public sectors, as evidenced by the fact that President George W. Bush appointed him to the Private Sector Senior Advisory Committee of the Homeland Security Advisory Council in 2004. Bill's zeal to keep our country's citizens protected continues as he now addresses how to prevent one of our country's most tragic challenges—the rising incidences of workplace violence across the United States.

But Whitmore understands that there is more to workplace safety than physical security. Tragic shootings at Columbine, Virginia Tech, Fort Hood and in workplaces across the country, along with such high-profile incidents as the small plane into the Internal Revenue Service office building in Austin, Texas in 2010, are increasingly focusing our collective consciousness on a critical aspect of workplace safety that extends beyond the physical, centered on the core cultures of our organizations.

And that's why this book belongs on the desk of every c-suite executive, department head, security manager and HR professional, regardless of the size of their organization. While there are plenty of books on workplace violence prevention from academics and researchers, this is the only one that offers real world perspective and counsel by the leader of America's #1 physical security company.

Whitmore believes that "workplace violence arises from deep-seated forces that live within many human beings. In the right mix of circumstances, pressures, and social dynamics someone may snap and a violent action or actions will take place. There simply is no magic formula that dictates who the perpetrator is, where the violent event takes place, or who the victims will turn out to be. For every 'typical' perpetrator profile, there are outliers. For every common office attack, there are upscale corporate suites where incidents of violence erupt. Victims of workplace violence come from all walks of life."

In these pages, Whitmore demonstrates how a broad range of people— including executives, law enforcement, contract security, human resources and building management personnel—can collectively build a culture of engagement, empowerment and education to lower an organization's workplace violence risk. He explains how everyone in an organization has a responsibility to be an active participant in stopping workplace violence before it happens. Employees are not apt to act on this kind of mandate just because management rolls out an unguided decree that "if you see something, say something." Whitmore educates the reader on how one can effectively act on that motto with the appropriate education, awareness and organizational support.

The ultimate truth is this: None of us can be passive observers to our own safety. Educating, engaging and empowering every person to observe and then act is an essential key to our organizational security and success.

Acknowledgements

Writing a book is a major project, and I couldn't have done it alone. This has truly been a team effort, and I have many people to acknowledge for their valuable contributions.

Thanks, first, to my valued industry colleagues, who were instrumental in bringing their real-world perspectives and decades of expertise to the book, including Bonnie Michelman, Maureen Rush, Patrick Wolfe, Chris Swecker, Steven Crimando and Don Bitner.

I also owe my gratitude to the knowledgeable AlliedBarton executives who contributed to the book, including David Buckman, Doug Fogwell, Larry Loesch, Rich Cordivari, Mike Meehan, Mimi Lanfranchi, Rich Michau, Ron Rabena, Jim Gillece, Glenn Rosenberg, Bill Tate, Mike Coleman, Charlie Bohenberger, Bob Chartier and Ken Bukowski.

Dr. Mortimer Feinberg continues to contribute his valuable insights on how people work with one another and the dynamics of today's organizations.

Nancy Tamosaitis at Vorticom brought her communications talent to this project, as did AlliedBarton's internal marketing communications team, which includes Alan Stein and Samantha Thomas.

For their book development and publishing expertise I'd like to thank Michael Roney and his team at Highpoint Executive Publishing, including Michael Utvich, Sarah M. Clarehart, Maureen Moriarty and Michael D. Welch.

David Michaelson contributed valuable survey and statistical analysis expertise, while Brandon Griggs and his colleagues at SiteStrux applied their talents to the book's website, found at www.potentialthebook.com.

Thanks always to my executive assistant, Kimberly Gardner, who skillfully keeps our projects moving smoothly amid competing schedules and other complexities.

Thanks to the men and women of AlliedBarton Security Services who take the lead every day, making the workplace safe and secure. I truly appreciate their dedication.

Finally, I'd like to acknowledge the steadfast support of my wife and family throughout this project.

Security and Potential

Potential is everywhere, both good and bad.

Take Google, for example. It was incorporated in a Menlo Park, California garage in 1998. When its 2004 IPO offered shares at $85, many skeptics thought that the valuation was high. Yet Google broke $100 on the first day, soared past $700 in 2007 and has been trading north of $400 ever since—all due to its founders' ability to recognize market needs and think outside of the box.

Starbucks originally opened as a local Seattle coffee house in 1971. Since then it has radically changed the way the world consumes coffee, as well as the business models of scores of companies that have followed. Thanks to creative ideas and a strong corporate culture, Starbucks now boasts more than 17,000 stores in 50 countries.

These examples obviously reflect the good kind of potential, but there's another, darker type as well: The potential for workplace violence in your organization. Before you protest that it's not likely to happen at your workplace, just consider the following:

+ The Occupational Safety and Health Administration (OSHA) reports that approximately two million Americans are victims of workplace violence each year, costing businesses up to $120 billion annually.

+ Almost 50 percent of all businesses have had at least one violent event, according to Extreme Behavioral Risk Management Inc. (XBRM).

- ✦ Homicide remains the leading cause of death for women in the workplace.

- ✦ Every day an average of two people are killed and 87 injured as a result of a workplace violence incident, according to the United States Bureau of Labor Statistics.

- ✦ A nationwide workplace violence survey that AlliedBarton conducted in May 2011 found that one in three Americans employed outside the home are "very" or "somewhat concerned" with their personal safety.

Not a pretty picture. However, despite these grim statistics, the number of people who have died from workplace shootings actually has been dropping for more than a decade, according to the U.S. Department of Labor. Much of this decline is attributed to increased employee awareness, training and faster and better medical response.

That's good to know. Now here's some additional positive news: Many of the same values and practices that can give your organization the potential to perform like Google or Starbucks at its peak are the same as those that will help protect it from violent incidents.

So, it would appear that there is some hope after all for staunching the violence that traumatizes millions and saps the reputations and success of so many organizations. That's why I wrote this book.

A Pressing Issue for Every Organization

As illustrated by all of those disturbing statistics, the prevention of workplace violence is consistently reported as one of the top issues facing corporate America, as it is in government entities, higher education and nonprofit associations.

Workplace violence is an especially critical issue for those charged with corporate security. Every year Pinkerton Consulting surveys Fortune 1000 security executives to determine their most pressing concerns. Workplace violence prevention has ranked at the very top of the list in every year since 1997 except for 1998 and 2010, when it placed second. Other concerns included threat assessments, strategic planning, implementing best practices, training effectiveness and employee background checks.

When asked in 2010 to rank their top security challenges on a scale of 5 (most important) to 1 (least important), these same executives cited employee awareness as their greatest concern, with threat assessment,

Top Security Management Challenges

Rank	Security Issues	Score
1	Promoting Employee Awareness	3.78
2 (tie)	Threat Assessments	3.71
2 (tie)	Minimizing Return on Investment	3.71
4	Strategic Planning	3.70
5	Implementing Best Practice/Stadards/Key Performance Indicators	3.68
6	Keeping up with Technological Advances	3.59
7	Adequate Security Staffing	3.58
8	Training Effectiveness/Methods	3.57
9	Employee Background Checks	3.54
10	Financial Management	3.48

Source: Securitas Security Services USA

Most security management challenges relate directly to organizational culture.

strategic planning, security staffing, training effectiveness and background checks also seen as critical areas of focus. (The chart on this page shows the overall rankings.)

All of these concerns can be linked directly with organizational culture and the imperative of leadership to instill and nourish the values and systems to support adequate safeguards.

Indeed, this culture needs to permeate the organization on every level—not only in recognizing the reality that workplace violence can happen anywhere, but also from understanding that fully developing the professional and personal potential of employees will place the organization in a better position for prevention and overall success.

Unfortunately, we have found that an extremely wide gap separates the perception of how employees see their organizations dealing with the issues of workplace violence and how the c-suite handles both prevention and response.

A Costly Problem

OSHA's 2011 workplace violence fact sheet has stated it clearly: 5,900 people killed in workplace homicides in the last 10 years, representing the third leading cause of death for people at work. That's startling enough, but you must also factor in the general consensus within the security professional community that this figure actually has been suppressed by the enhancement of emergency medical care and its ability to save lives.

According to this same fact sheet, it is 100 times more costly to react to an incident versus preventing one. This is a staggering number, and the main source of that cost of $120 billion a year to American businesses. Clearly, this is a costly problem.

Protecting Your Investment

As the CEO of a company with roughly 55,000 employees, I am keenly aware of the need to focus on programs and practices to mitigate the issue. I have an added stake in this as well: When you look at the statistics of who was a victim of workplace violence, law enforcement and security are high up on the list. After all, those on the front lines of protecting people and property of the residential communities, businesses and communities we serve have the greatest exposure to the problem. This means that I've had to personally call the families of our employees who have been killed in the line of duty. So perhaps I have felt the repercussions of workplace violence to an even greater degree than most corporate CEOs, and that makes me all the more determined to do something about it, and help you and your organization deal with it as well.

It's imperative that we put this issue front and center. It's something we all have to address as an integrated part of our organizational strategy—one that starts in the c-suite and permeates down through every level of the company.

Addressing the Threat

Here's a statistic that's amazing to me: According to the National Institute for Occupational Safety and Health, more than 70 percent of U.S. workplaces do not have a formal program or policy in place to address workplace violence. That's pretty astounding considering the statistics, the ongoing threats that exist in the workplace and the concern that we hear from corporate security executives year after year.

Many security professionals have been trained to recognize potential workplace violence behavior, but that's clearly not enough. Every employee—from security pros and c-suite business leaders, to middle managers, line managers and support staff alike—has a critical role in building a workplace violence prevention culture and educating those within our organizations to recognize workplace violence trigger points, or markers. Creating this kind of corporate culture—one that promotes, "if you see something, say something"—can have lifesaving consequences and enhance the smooth, profitable performance of any organization.

I recently spent some quality time with a number of chief security officers from various industries. One of them remarked that workplace violence prevention does not really make for a "feel good" poster that you can put on the walls of your office. Well, that may seem to be true on first consideration, but there are different ways to approach the issue. One corporation I'm aware of is coming up with a branding or naming campaign to focus on words other than "workplace violence" and still get the message across. It's an issue that has to be front and center, even if it initially makes you uncomfortable.

AlliedBarton has sponsored workplace violence prevention programs all over the country. We do seminars all the time, and they usually are well attended. This is my 30th year with the company, and I have never previously seen the type of attendance that we are getting at these events. The fact that these programs draw a crowd illustrates the fact that this is a hot-button issue for many.

So why do 70 percent of corporations still not have a formal program? Maybe it's that fear of using the words—workplace violence. Maybe it's the lack of understanding about what workplace violence really is, or how to actually go about implementing a prevention program. What are the underpinning values, best practices and structure? I address all of those considerations in this book.

Nevertheless, any discussion about workplace violence cannot be complete without acknowledging certain limitations about what can be done to prevent it. Throughout this book, I outline an approach aimed at preventing incidents in your organization. However, the nature of workplace violence is such that even the most prepared organization may still be a victim of it.

Understanding Workplace Violence

Here's some more positive news: After years of monitoring workplace violence, we have a base of expertise and understanding of the patterns of incidents, the types of behavior, and the "typical" perpetrators. This base of knowledge is the foundation for any organization that wishes to build an effective response and help secure itself against the threats of workplace violence in the future. It's also the main topic of Chapter 1, though I touch on it here.

What's really important is to understand specifically what "workplace violence" means beyond the superficial understandings put forth in the media and everyday usage. If you say "workplace violence" to the average person, 99 times out of 100 they immediately will think of the classic media "going postal" story, where the enraged or disgruntled employee, often recently fired, takes a gun back into his or her workplace to take out his manager and other coworkers as well. Regrettably, this scenario has been acted out on national television enough times and in enough different places to become almost a cliché. But violence in the workplace—your day-to-day workplace—is something much less dramatic and life threatening. For example:

- Workplace violence is any physical assault, threatening behavior, or verbal abuse occurring in the work setting.

- Ninety seven percent of workplace acts of violence are nonfatal, ranging from sexual harassment, verbal threats and bullying to fistfights.

So, on an everyday level workplace violence is much more mundane than the "going postal" stories you hear in the media. It's often about conflicts and intensity that exceed the acceptable forms of business interaction, though these very same acts can escalate to more violent forms.

Building a Secure, High-Performance Organization

Building a secure and high-performance organization is about a lot more than guarding against that rare but catastrophic active shooter event at one of your worksites. It is about the challenge of building a prevention culture where every employee is educated, engaged and enabled to recognize the early-warning signs of workplace violence and then take action. This requires making daily distinctions, between what is acceptable business behavior—the normal standard interaction that is acceptable in business—and an unacceptable level of violence, threat, intimidation and bullying that has the potential to escalate and accelerate to something much darker and more dangerous.

Building Leadership

Proactive leadership in the face of workplace violence potential is essential to implementing a prevention program, building a prevention culture and making it effective. In fact, I would go as far as to say that creating effective leadership at all levels of the organization is by far the largest and most critical challenge in the effort.

Workplace violence prevention through leadership starts at the top and involves everyone in the organization. Leadership qualities can be embodied by any employee at any level. This is particularly important in an organization such as ours, where our many account-level employees are directly charged with securing the people, property and assets of our customers. Making this work, in my opinion, means providing continual training and learning opportunities to ensure that leadership values are embraced at all levels of our company.

Engaging Employees

In large part, workplace violence prevention is about engaged employees. The more engaged an employee, the more likely that person will point out a potential perpetrator. An engaged employee is the first line of defense, and if you're not paying attention to this, it could cost you as a company. At a minimum, it is essential that all employees understand that they play an active role in workplace violence prevention. Education and awareness are critical parts of this effort, and that, along with leadership, is a core focus of this book. The daily interactions of coworkers weigh heavily on the ability to identify potential issues before they become disasters, and your employees must be aware of the warning signs and know where to go for help.

Implementing Next Practices

Effective workplace violence prevention also requires implementing what can be called next practices, the commitment to not just doing what has worked in the past, but committing to forward-looking practices that address our security needs now and tomorrow.

Workplace violence prevention plans cannot afford to be stagnant, because the dynamics of the workplace change quickly. Modern technology and public/private partnerships with law enforcement and private security create a great synergy. Any prevention program, any training or education program, should clearly take advantage of diverse opportunities and opinions by bringing expertise together from the public and the private sectors.

Indeed, one of the most important steps businesses can take is get in contact with local law enforcement agencies and their security team to work together on preventative planning. That will help ensure that everyone knows what to expect and what to do if workplace harassment or violence occurs.

The integrated training and resources of the public and private security sectors aids in the facilitation of management training to help recognize the behaviors and symptoms of disgruntled workers that can lead to harassment, bullying and deadly active-shooter scenarios.

I served for five years on the Private Sector Senior Advisory Committee of the Homeland Security Advisory Council—some called it "the private sector of Homeland Security" because we were all nongovernment employees. Collaborating with CEOs from major U.S. companies was incredibly interesting to me, especially from the perspective of the powerful dynamics of the public and private sectors working together to come up with best practices. The dynamic does work.

How to Use this Book

I've structured this book to assist you in building your own high-potential workplace violence prevention culture, based on the core principles of leadership, employee engagement and next practices. Creating an effective program is a multi-disciplinary challenge, requiring clearly articulated values and the formal programs to support and nurture them. Throughout all of this book's chapters, I use AlliedBarton's own programs as examples and models that you can consider for your own needs.

Here's how I've structured the book:

Part One: Cost and Opportunity

I begin by laying out the baselines for understanding what is and isn't workplace violence, and then suggest ways in which you can think about these realities in a manner that will pave the way for practices and policies to benefit your organization. This part includes the following chapter topics:

- **What Is Workplace Violence…Really?:** Workplace violence comes from a range of sources and occurs in several levels of gradation. Being fully aware of these shades of workplace violence, and making sure that your employees also understand them, is the first step in securing your organization.

- **Five Myths that Could Land Your Company in Trouble:** The general understanding of workplace violence is full of myths. Accepting these myths can come back to haunt you.

→ **Embracing the Cold Hard Truths:** Once you clear the air of all the smokescreens and misconceptions that have grown up around workplace violence, you can begin to focus on the facts. From those facts you can begin to properly understand what this phenomenon is, and how it truly affects us.

→ **Establishing "Next Practices" for Your Organization:** We need ways to stretch our thinking and anticipate future events not yet seen, so in this chapter I discuss future planning and strategic thinking through what are increasingly being called next practices.

Part Two: Enabling Your Secure Organization

This part is really the heart of the book. Here I drill down into what I see as the four core factors that must be activated to build a safe, secure organizational culture. Chapter topics include the following:

→ **Begin with Leadership:** Strong and steady leadership lies at the heart of workplace violence prevention. Establishing leadership principles and extending them to every employee is a major factor in making your organization more secure and successful overall.

→ **Nurture Employee Engagement:** A way to help prevent workplace violence is to get employees engaged. More engaged employees will lower workplace violence.

→ **Encourage Individual Growth:** If you value a safe and secure work environment, you need to spend the time, effort and money to be sure that every employee has the very best opportunity to reach his or her full potential.

→ **Make Workplace Violence Prevention Everybody's Job:** Everybody in the company has a responsibility of leadership from the perspective of being observant. Educating, engaging and empowering every employee to observe and act is an essential key to your security.

Part Three: Applying Next Practices for Success

In this final part of the book I discuss how to put all of the previously discussed concepts and practices together to create an effective workplace violence prevention program. The topics covered here are as follows:

→ **Strategies for a Secure, High-Performance Organization:** Putting a comprehensive workplace violence prevention program into place combines all of the understandings, high-level concepts and next practices described in this book.

* **Securing Healthcare:** Despite the warm sounding name, the healthcare industry is the business of life and death, where a combination of intense pressure, high emotions, the presence of drugs and alcohol can create an explosive mix. Here I look at this sector's special considerations.

* **Looking Ahead to a Secure, Successful Future:** In this final chapter I touch on some of the issues that have formed the core of this book, with a perspective on the workplace security challenges and opportunities that face all of us going forward.

Special Features

Most of this book's chapters include special editorial features that are designed to add depth and dimension to your understanding of workplace violence prevention. These include the following:

* **Roundtable:** In May 2011 I gathered some of the country's top security leaders for an in-depth discussion of the threats, challenges and remedies for workplace violence from their unique perspectives. Segments of this discussion appear in each chapter in order to add some industry-specific depth and perspective to the topic. Industries represented include higher education, healthcare, insurance and banking.

* **Guest Expert:** At the end of each chapter you'll find the perspectives of an internal AlliedBarton specialist who gives an expert technical or operational perspective on the topic.

Overall, this book is designed so that you can drop in anywhere and come away with some valuable information. However, I believe that you'll get the most from it if you read it from beginning to end.

The Time to Act Is Now

Violence should not be part of the workplace; awareness and prevention should. I applaud you for picking up this book because the first step to keeping your company safe is what you are doing now: learning more about workplace violence prevention so that you can put effective programs into practice at your organization.

Unfortunately, in today's environment, no business or industry is immune to the possibility of workplace violence, terrorism or any number of manmade or natural disasters. The all-too-frequent media reports of armed attackers in our workplaces should be enough to discourage an ostrich-like approach. The time to act is clearly now, and all organizations need to focus on prevention. Actively addressing this topic is essential to the safety and livelihood of your business.

Ultimately, leadership and awareness are key to reaching your potential as a safe and successful organization, and your proactive preparations for events considered unimaginable can save lives. So, let's get started.

Part One
Cost and Opportunity

chapter 1

What is Workplace Violence... Really?

On September 1, 2010, in Silver Springs, Maryland, a disturbed man named James Jae Lee walked into the lobby of a major media company's headquarters with a pipe bomb, four propane tanks and an oxygen tank strapped to his chest. For years previously, Lee had mounted a venomous and unhinged campaign of web posts blaming the company for offering programming that, at least in his mind, promoted overpopulation. He was carrying a switch intended to detonate the bomb if he let go, but fortunately the device didn't explode when he fell to the ground after being shot by a SWAT team that had been summoned to the scene.

Different Shades of Violence

This is the typical public impression of workplace violence—a disgruntled customer or employee going off the deep end, "going postal" and wreaking havoc—perhaps even killing someone. Horrific events like the ones that took place at Columbine, Virginia Tech, Fort Hood and Tucson also play into the typical public association. Of course, these incidents are indeed workplace violence in its most dramatic and potentially catastrophic form. However, it's essential to understand that workplace violence is so much more than just the guy with a bomb strapped to his chest, or a former employee or deranged student charging into a building or a crowd with a gun in his hand. Workplace violence comes from a range of sources and occurs in several levels of gradation. Becoming fully aware of these shades of workplace violence is the first step in securing your organization, and is the main topic of this chapter.

Violent Intent

Let me return briefly to the guy in Silver Springs, who obviously was intent on perpetrating workplace violence in one of its most violent forms. After entering the lobby of the building, James Jae Lee took two employees and a security officer hostage. An off-duty officer, one of the first on the scene, spotted Lee, then walked around the large building to another entrance— one that ultimately was used by the SWAT teams when they responded to a call for help. A contingent of officers soon arrived at the scene, secured the company's security control room and proceeded to describe all they observed to commanders stationed outside. Employees were evacuated safely, and Lee wasn't able to go anywhere else in the building.

Negotiations with Lee followed. "I have nothing else to live for," he stated. Asked what he meant, he said, "This is it. This is the end, all right?" Ultimately, the officers inside the building decided to confront Lee, despite the bomb that was strapped to his torso. Two teams of eight covertly positioned themselves in the lobby, and they moved in as soon as the two civilian hostages ran out the front door. They then shot and disabled Lee in a precisely choreographed attack.

Although Lee had previously lived in homeless shelters, police discovered that he had been renting a room in the Wheaton area and searched his home the day after the hostage crisis. They found a calendar on his computer with Sept. 1 marked as "The End."

Fortunately, none of the employees at this company's headquarters were seriously injured or killed that day, but the gunman did lose his life—not the best conclusion.

Cool Heads and Speedy Action

Here's another incident. On a partly cloudy day in May 2011, time passed in a quiet and ordinary manner for our security team at a mall in the northeast—at least until just after 5:00 p.m. At that hour, Security Dispatcher David Domenico was on duty monitoring cameras in the closed circuit television room. During a routine "camera patrol" of the parking garage's upper level, he noticed a man walking towards one of the facility's walls. The man's actions seemed unusual, so Domenico watched closely as the subject stopped and appeared to stare at the ledge. Thinking he might be watching a person contemplating suicide, he radioed several officers to come to the scene. He observed the subject take off his shoes and climb on the ledge. The man sat with his legs straddling both sides and dropped something onto the ground below. Domenico passed this information along to the officers now en route.

Assistant Security Director Tim Patterson heard the radio call and responded to the scene, bringing three additional officers as part of a special response team. He soon arrived and took charge, accompanied by a local police officer who was working an off-duty detail for the mall. As they approached the subject, Patterson engaged the man in a conversation while he and the policeman edged ever closer. Once they felt that they were close enough to take action safely, they grabbed the man's leg so that he could not jump. He then was restrained for his own protection until EMS and law enforcement officers arrived, as Domenico had already called 911. The municipal fire department appeared within a few minutes and took the subject into custody. We later learned that this man suffered from a number of mental health issues and was under the care of a physician, but had stopped taking his medication.

Thanks to his extraordinary observation skills, Domenico was able to get an AlliedBarton team of security officers and police to the scene before this distressed individual could jump. Patterson and the other officers assisting him used exemplary judgment in approaching and restraining the subject in a way that didn't endanger them. And thanks to the cool heads, quick action and keen professionalism of the AlliedBarton officers involved, Friday the 13th turned out to be a lucky day for this potential suicide victim.

Predictable Behavior

Back in October 1985, a 25-year old woman dressed in military fatigues opened fire with a semi-automatic rifle at a mall outside of Philadelphia, killing three people, including a two-year-old, and wounding seven others before being disarmed by a shopper. In all she fired 20 rounds, and at the time she was stopped she had 10 bullets left in one of her clips.

The shooter, Silvia Seegrist, had been diagnosed as schizophrenic 10 years earlier. She had been committed and discharged from mental health facilities several times. In recent months she had repeatedly exhibited disturbing behavior in and around the mall. For example, she would often show up there wearing green Army fatigues, crouching in firing positions, and randomly going up to other shoppers and expressing approval, even excitement, about other killing sprees she had learned about on the news.

In the days leading up to the incident she had tried to purchase a rifle at a local KMart and was turned away, but finally got what she needed at another store.

When she randomly opened fire that day as she walked down the mall's corridors, people at first didn't believe she was shooting a real gun. Workplace violence at the time was not prominent in their minds, and most did not associate women with those kinds of crimes. Once it became clear that this military-clad individual was actually shooting real bullets, shoppers ducked down or ran for cover. However, nobody tried to intervene until a 24-year-old graduate student, assuming she was causing a ruckus by shooting blanks, grabbed her and summoned a security officer. She did resist, but allowed herself to be directed to a bench, where she and her captor awaited the arrival of authorities.

When asked why she did it, she simply replied "My family makes me nervous."

In retrospect, this was a case where all of the warning signs were painfully obvious, yet there was no protocol or program for recognizing these signs and taking action to intervene. The attorney who represented the mall visited with my company at a later date and spoke about lessons learned. What could they have done differently? Clearly, someone should have intervened earlier in response to this woman's behavior.

Bullying and Sexual Harassment

Not all incidents of workplace violence are so dramatic as the preceding cases, though they nonetheless cause damage even if they don't lead to more violent acts.

Here's an example. The number-two person at one of our client sites was a bully, and many of our employees became a victim to that bullying, along with most of the other workers with whom he came in contact. When a supervisor bullies people, it can bring down the morale and productivity of everyone who is in his or her sphere. In this case, which is typical, there was a widespread attitude at the site of "Woe is me! What can I do?" or a resigned and somewhat hopeless "It's just the way it is." There was nobody standing up to this guy. There was high employee turnover and a real lack of engagement. We advised this client that they had to make a change, and they took our report very seriously. The employees at this site already had suffered through years of humiliation resulting in high turnover and poor service.

In another example, we discovered that there was a lawsuit on the books of an acquisition target about a client demanding sex from one of the female employees in order for her to keep her job. Litigation resulted, and it ended up costing a lot of money—and that's in addition to the adverse emotional impact that this behavior had on not only the victim—but on many other employees there. The worst part of the case was that one female complained repeatedly and no one helped her. Clearly, this also is workplace violence.

Warning Signs and Intervention

Recognition and intervention can be critical in helping to prevent workplace violence at all levels. Consider what happened unexpectedly on another day when a disgruntled employee, upset by his termination from a manufacturing facility, began sending letters to the CEO and attempted to visit his former workplace. Mimi Lanfranchi, who now is AlliedBarton's Senior Vice President, National Accounts and Specialized Services, was working as a security consultant for that company at the time. She reports that the company contacted local law enforcement authorities, who got involved and repeatedly arrested the man. The disgruntled former employee's behavior reflective of an emotionally troubled individual and was very distressing to the CEO.

The company's concern continued and so its staff reached out for help to further address the problem. Through an investigative process including background checks and surveillance, they determined that the man was somewhat unbalanced and had no financial or family support system to help him.

As part of the solution process, the company asked Mimi to contact this troubled man in hopes of de-escalating the situation and his hostility toward his former employer. The company told him that Mimi was a third party consultant hired to help him get back on track. Mimi and the man spoke on numerous occasions over a three-week period where they slowly shifted the conversation from his dissatisfaction with his previous employer to a more positive focus on the future which included providing him with avenues for finding a new job.

So What Is Workplace Violence?

As illustrated in the incidents I've described here, workplace violence and its precursors can take on many different forms. While news coverage of workplace shootings tends to define the typical public understanding, its true nature is far broader. Shootings represent the extreme apex of vicious acts, but workplace violence is also defined as threats and other intimidation or harassing behavior directed toward a person at work. This is critical to keep in mind: Many less-dramatic levels of inappropriate or abusive behavior are in their own measure forms of workplace violence, and these can lead to more destructive manifestations.

The 2011 Report on Workplace Violence published by the Institute of Management and Administration (IOMA) defines workplace violence events as generally falling into one of the following four types of situations:

* **Criminal.** When the perpetrator has no legitimate relationship to the business or its employees and is usually committing a crime in conjunction with the violence (e.g., robbery, shoplifting, or trespassing).

* **Customer or client.** When the perpetrator has a legitimate relationship with the business and becomes violent while being served by the business (e.g., customers, clients, patients, students, inmates, or any other group to which the business provides services).

* **Coworker.** When the perpetrator is an employee of the business, past employee or contractor who works as a temporary employee of the business and attacks or threatens another employee.

* **Domestic violence.** When the perpetrator has no legitimate relationship to the business but has a personal relationship with the intended victim, who is an employee.

I'd add one more category to this widely accepted list:

* **Terrorist/True Believer:** This is a person with a nearly fanatical devotion to a cause—blind dedication that causes that individual to throw normal social norms out the window, causing destruction or even harm to a real or perceived enemy, or those who may not agree with his or her point of view.

Yet as I illustrated earlier, these perpetrator categories are only part of the story. Workplace violence also is defined by levels of behavior.

The Gradations of Workplace Violence

According to ASIS International, workplace violence refers to a broad range of behaviors falling along a spectrum that, due to their nature and/or severity, significantly affect the workplace, generates a concern for personal safety, or results in physical injury or death. Milder behaviors include any disruptive, aggressive, hostile or emotionally abusive behaviors. Midrange behaviors demonstrate direct, conditional or veiled threats, stalking and aggressive harassment. Violent behaviors include overt violence causing physical injury, but every level has a cost, whether it is a degradation of your organization's cultural ethic, low morale, high turnover, lower productivity, and so on.

This range of behaviors has been linked to the more dramatic and destructive forms of workplace violence. In a 2004 *USA Today* analysis of 224 fatal incidents of workplace violence, the attacker often had left behind clear warning signs. A national survey on workplace bullying from Zogmy International found that about 54 million Americans report being bullied at work with an estimated 43,800 acts of harassment, bullying and other threatening behavior occurring in the workplace every day.

In our own national survey, conducted in May 2011, we found that more than half of Americans employed outside their homes (52 percent) have witnessed, heard about, are aware of or have experienced a violent event or an event that could lead to violence at their workplace. These events include open hostility, abusive language or threats and can escalate up to the infliction of significant physical harm to someone by another person.

There are in some cases warning signs for an employee who requires intervention, and as leaders who guide the fortunes of our organizations, we need to make sure all employees understand and recognize the more subtle forms of workplace violence—the warning signs of potentially destructive acts to come—so that everyone can act as eyes and ears to recognize and report unusual behavior.

Introducing the Workplace Violence Continuum

How many times after a workplace violence incident have you heard people say "We knew that he was going to go off eventually" or "We were afraid of him"? Jared Lee Loughner, the deeply disturbed individual in Arizona who stands accused of shooting Congresswoman Gabby Gifford and killing six other people, including a federal judge, is a case in point. People from nearly every facet of his life recalled odd, off-putting and ominous behavior. A college professor even wrote that he was afraid of Loughner in the classroom. In this case, the college raised warning flags and kicked him out of the school, but ultimately there was no intervention prior to the shooter's senseless act.

To be fair, there are many instances in which those who knew an actor of workplace violence profess how peaceful, normal or friendly he or she seemed to be. But where the signs are clear, action can and should be taken.

Workplace violence usually is tied to a broad range of behaviors that often can predict more severe actions. These behaviors fall along a spectrum that, depending on their nature or severity, significantly affect the workplace, generate a concern for personal safety, and/or result in physical injury or even death. All of the scenarios we and others in our industry have identified occur frequently in workplaces across the country.

Any employee with one or more of the following indicators may be in need of assistance. Managers must be alert to these indirect pleas for help and provide a positive and timely response to ensure a safe and secure work environment.

1. **Unusual Behavior:** This can range from uncharacteristic excessive absences or tardiness by a normally punctual employee, to changes in performance, work habits or attitude.

2. **Inappropriate Acting Out:** Saying highly inappropriate things to people, getting very upset at colleagues, pouting, refusing to participate in meetings or work tasks, slamming doors, throwing things, etc. Resistance and overreaction to changes in policy and procedures. Increased severe mood swings, noticeably unstable, emotional responses and testing the limits of supervisors' authority and control.

3. **Verbal Assault:** Explosive outbursts of anger/rage, insulting or shouting at colleagues without provocation.

4. **Harassment:** Saying highly inappropriate things. Sexually aggressive behavior or sexual harassment, stalking, etc.

5. **Threatening Behavior:** Actually making threats verbally or with hands or objects. Threatening emails, memos, etc. Brandishing a weapon at the workplace.

6. **Physical Assault:** Lashing out physically or actually attacking someone.

Workplace Violence Continuum

AlliedBarton's Workplace Violence Continuum

7. **Deadly encounter:** This is usually manifested as the classic active shooter scenario, a most tragic culmination of all that has come before.

Remember that just because someone exhibits one of these behaviors does not necessarily mean they are prone to acts of violence. It is when someone has an uncharacteristic, noticeable change in behavior, when that behavior is displayed constantly, or when uncharacteristic behaviors are observed in combination, that you should consider telling someone in a position of authority about the situation.

Recognizing the Warning Signs

The beginning of the pathway to all of these forms of workplace violence can often be recognized. You just have to look for the typical warning signs signaling that something is seriously amiss. These include the following:

+ **Excessive tardiness or absences:** An employee who consistently leaves their workday early without authorization, or presents numerous excuses for shortening the workday, should set off an alarm. This is a significant sign for an individual who is typically prompt and committed to a full workday.

* **Uncharacteristic need for supervision:** Generally, an employee requires less supervision as he or she becomes more proficient at his or her work. An employee who exhibits an increased or uncharacteristic need for supervision, or with whom the supervisor must spend an inordinate amount of time, may be an individual who is signaling a need for help. Managers should be alert to such a change and consider offering professional intervention if needed.

* **Lack of performance:** If an employee who is normally efficient and productive experiences a sudden or sustained drop in performance, you have reason for concern. This is actually a classic warning sign of dissatisfaction, and the manager should meet with the employee immediately to determine a mutually beneficial course of action.

* **Change in work habits:** As in the case of reduced productivity, an employee exhibiting inconsistent work habits may be in need of intervention. If you think about your peers at work, they are typically quite consistent in their work habits. If habits change, the manager has reason to suspect that the individual needs of assistance and that action should be taken.

* **Inability to concentrate:** If an employee is suddenly unable to concentrate, this may indicate that they are distracted and in trouble. A manager should be notified to try and encourage the employee to seek assistance.

* **Signs of stress:** If an employee who has traditionally adhered to safety procedures is suddenly involved in accidents or safety violations, this is often a sign that the employee is under a large degree of stress, which can be a significant contributor to workplace violence.

* **Change in attitude:** A sustained change in behavior often indicates an employee in difficulty. People are typically familiar with the personalities of their peers and quickly to notice major changes. Your work environment should be managed to ensure trust and open communication.

* **Weapons fascination:** A classic behavioral warning sign is someone who is fascinated with weapons. This should be easily recognized and reported.

✦ **Drugs and alcohol:** A person's mood or character often changes when drugs or alcohol are used. Often people who have substance abuse problems act out in the workplace, and it's important that every organization have some methodology in place to identify and assist victims of drug or alcohol abuse.

✦ **Not taking responsibility for actions:** A person who uses excuses and blames others is a classic behavioral warning sign that is easy to identify but just as often ignored by managers. A worker who engages in this behavior is typically signaling for assistance and may require counseling.

These are only a few of the possible warning signs of workplace violence. As with any work-related issue, you should report highly unusual behavior to a manager or someone who has the authority to take action.

Challenges in Preventing Workplace Violence

None of us is perfect, nor is any warning system fail-safe. The simple reality is that otherwise peaceful, stable performers sometimes suddenly snap without any real warning. Sure, there may be a precipitating event in the moments or hours before the violent outburst, but these events and an individual's reaction may be nearly impossible to anticipate. In such circumstances, the workplace violence is not preventable by anyone, even with perfect knowledge of the actor's situation.

The danger lies in believing that simply because some incidents of workplace violence are impossible to prevent—or as I discuss below, that they are difficult to prevent—all workplace violence is impossible to prevent. Though some professionals may disagree as to whether few, some or most incidents of workplace violence are avoidable, the disagreement is beside the point. Certainly, some instances of workplace violence are preventable, and organizational leaders would be well-served to acknowledge it, and take measures to prevent it.

It's Hard to Prevent Workplace Violence.

It would be naïve to assert that preventing workplace violence was a simple matter of implementing the practices outlined in the chapters that follow. In reality, guarding against workplace violence is hard for a number of reasons that result from societal, human, and legal factors.

As will be discussed in the following chapters, an organization's ability to identify those at risk of engaging in violence in the workplace largely depends on our knowledge of, and familiarity with, our coworkers. Yet our social norms are in conflict with this objective. In the United States, we live in an open, free and largely safe society. We value our personal independence, resilience and most importantly, our personal privacy. More so than ever before, I see employees maintaining strict separation of their "work" and "personal" lives, leaving leaders uninformed about whatever personal issues may create a risk of workplace violence. Moreover, U.S. culture and laws have long protected an individual's right to own and carry a firearm, which by way of observation and not opinion elevates the risk of catastrophic incidents of workplace violence.

The nature of human interaction also complicates identifying those behaviors described in the Workplace Violence Continuum. I personally believe that people are understanding, accepting and generally want to "get along" with their colleagues. For the right reasons, we teach our children that "different" is not only acceptable, but a good thing. So when individuals are "different" in the workplace, there is a tendency to accept them as "quirky" or unique. When an employee experiences personal difficulty, he or she not only tries to keep it confidential from coworkers, the coworkers often want to be "understanding" and are reluctant to create a disciplinary situation out of their colleague's difficulties. There is an understandable desire to help their colleague work through the situation and not aggravate the individual's anxiety with employment issues.

Finally, even if an organization is successful at identifying the milder forms of workplace violence, they are constrained by laws and employment arrangements that affect what actions can be implemented. Sometimes conflict in the workplace results from racial, religious or sexual orientation issues, all of which are impacted by federal and state law prohibiting discrimination. The Americans with Disabilities Act protects an individual with a "mental disability." The National Labor Relations Board and collective bargaining agreements affect how unionized employees can be disciplined in many circumstances. Some states have enacted statutes that protect employees from being disciplined or counseled based on certain "off duty" conduct. Obviously, no law or collective bargaining agreement inhibits an employer's ability to discipline or terminate an obviously violent or disruptive employee. But as I discuss in this book, the key to reducing the risk of workplace violence lies in how you respond to sometimes mild behavior, and in this respect, an employer's ability to take lawful action can be a difficult call.

After an incident of workplace violence, the dots seem all too easy to connect. The point I make here is that the complex web of social factors, human interaction and legal obligations may make it impossible, or at a minimum, extremely difficult to recognize a problem early enough. After all, careful action to prevent workplace violence is unlikely to affect the overall crime rate in our society, and the best we may be able to achieve is to move an otherwise unavoidable tragic event out of the workplace to another locale.

An Observation on Personal Responsibility

I discussed in the previous section the value our society places on individual responsibility. I write in this book about steps that an organization can take to reduce the risk of workplace violence affecting its employees and its brand. There remains a largely universal truth that requires mentioning here. Each individual is responsible for his or her own behavior. The individual who commits a heinous act of violence against another human being is the one responsible for its human toll. Maybe this point is obvious, but I offer it at the risk that anyone might conclude that I believe an organization is responsible for the criminally violent acts of an individual.

It is sad and perhaps ironic that there are certain workplace violence scenarios in which the individual victim of the violence was the one person who had the most knowledge of the pending threat, and had the greatest opportunity to prevent it. It may be regarded by some as preposterous or ignorant to "blame the victim." But I am not blaming the victim; I state categorically here that no one ever deserves to be the victim of violence. The point of this book is to reduce the likelihood that the violence ever occurs. A candid assessment of the facts leads to the foregoing statement.

The simple fact is that many instances of violence, workplace or otherwise, are motivated acts against known targets as opposed to random acts against unknown victims. Those closely affiliated with the perpetrator of the violence are more likely to know his or her mental state, violent propensities and physical whereabouts, and may be inclined to conceal those facts from their employer—or others. The scenario in which domestic abuse spills over to the workplace leaps to mind, but I am sure there are others.

ROUNDTABLE
Defining and Understanding Workplace Violence

Rich Cordivari, *Vice President, National Accounts, AlliedBarton Security Services*
Bonnie Michelman, *Director of Police and Outside Services, Massachusetts General Hospital*
Maureen Rush, *Vice President for Public Safety, University of Pennsylvania*
Chris Swecker, *former Assistant Director, Criminal Investigative Division, FBI*
Patrick J. Wolfe, *former Vice President for Corporate Security, CIGNA Corporation,
retired U.S. Secret Service*

Rich Cordivari: I have participated in at least a dozen workplace violence workshops in the past eight months or so. Requests are coming in for new sessions at least three or four times a week from our customers and prospects throughout the country. One of the common denominators in the vigorous Q&A afterwards, which dovetails on all of the points we've discussed so far, is "We know it's out there, but we are not sure what it is and we are not exactly sure what to do about it. Can you help us and provide guidance?" So, we want to bring in people like you who have an expert view of it, and especially from some of the industry sectors that we serve where we think there is a particular challenge.

Bonnie Michelman: I oversee about 400 people, 200 of which are licensed police officers. I have been in a variety of security positions at different industries prior to that. I teach part-time in the graduate school at Northeastern University and I do a lot of consulting in workforce violence nationally and abroad, and some risk assessments. I've also been president of ASIS and IHSS. The common denominator in all of the positions I've held is that workplace violence is perceived to be a major issue, but people don't know how to deal with it; they don't know how to set up preventions.

Chris Swecker: In a company of 300,000 the chance of an internal workplace violence issue is extremely high just based on sheer numbers of employees and contractors, so this potential scenario comes with the challenge of getting awareness at the highest levels so that you can sell your programs deeper into the organization. We need to do something about the prevailing culture at the management level. Community policing was successful because you could convince citizens to speak up—that hasn't found its way into the corporate culture and it's discouraging.

Michelson: Most companies are not going to have workplace violence in the going-postal way, so you need to redefine what it is, and really reinforce those definitions of threats of bullying, harassment, intimidation—they all have a fiscal impact, an operational impact and a liability impact that people can relate to in different ways. I think when you broaden people's definition of workplace violence, that's when you can get people to buy into it.

Patrick J. Wolfe: Corporations should foster a culture that prohibits disrespect and poor behavior. They should limit their risk of hiring employees with these traits by performing pre-employment drug testing and conducting employee background checks. This not only limits liability, but also keeps a positive atmosphere in the company.

Michelson: I think that what is going to help somewhat is the fact that within the next five years 95 percent of American companies will have a chief compliance officer. That may give some weight to this. We need consistent metrics and organization-to-organization definitions so that we have some basis for measuring it.

Maureen Rush: Domestic violence is not a code in the uniform crime reporting systems, and so for years police departments could never connect domestic violence with homicides. And then police departments started making subcategories so that they could track the cases and make correlations. It's the same thing with workplace violence. It could be an assault, but the terminologies are not compliant with how we code crimes. So if you don't code it, you don't track it, and you don't know what the true number is because there isn't a federal tracking system like there is for murder and other crimes.

Swecker: You know, the Bureau of Labor Statistics cites workplace violence as the third leading cause of death, but that includes retail robberies and retail violence, so one threshold question is does workplace violence include all of that or does it not? The countermeasures are different in these situations, as are the policies and strategies. You do need to be clear about the subsets we are talking about, because it's often a matter of fostering a culture of respect vs. straight-up security.

The Impact of Workplace Violence on the Organization

Beyond the tragic personal effect on victims, savvy business leaders understand the impact that a shooting could have on a brand's reputation, as well as the legal costs and declining employee morale and productivity that follow an incident. Even bullying behavior saps company efficiency, making a comprehensive workplace violence prevention program a bottom-line benefit to the organization. Our nationwide survey found that workers who experienced or are aware of violence or the conditions leading to violence at their workplace rate their current place of employment lower on every key measure than those haven't experienced these types of events, and that's got to affect performance.

The Cost of Inaction

In Chapter 2 I discuss the many fallacies that surround the topic of workplace violence—all misconceptions that can allow such events to happen, which then creates an adverse effect on the organization.

One of those misconceptions is the attitude of "it can't happen here," which is all too prevalent and fed by human nature. After all, if you're not aware of something currently happening, then it's easy to fall into that complacency of thinking everything is fine. I understand that it's easy not to take action when "nothing is happening." I also understand that in many organizations—maybe yours—it's difficult to dedicate time and resources (including training and financial investment) to something that's not blatantly apparent. It's also hard to convince the senior leadership to take action.

To effect change in a business, it might be helpful to articulate the need for action in financial terms. Poor morale, absenteeism, employee turnover and litigation—all effects of workplace violence on any level—can be costly indeed. Low morale directly relates to productivity, absenteeism and health care costs, not to mention behaviors that can cause more workplace violence issues. Consider the following:

→ According to a 2011 report by Health Populi, 51 percent of total health costs are attributed to lost productivity at work in terms of on-the-job performance and absence. The other 49 percent is made up of direct medical costs (27 percent) and wage replacements (22 percent). Thus, most health care costs to employers aren't in the medical care or insurance line item at all—they're in productivity.

* Stress from workplace violence can be expensive. The Health & Wellness Research Database published by the Canadian corporate consulting firm Shepell·fgi estimated in 2005 that the total value of lost work time due to stress amounted to $1.7 billion annually.

* The cost of turnover—training a new person in a job—is estimated by many sources to be about $60,000 per individual in a mid-range job, and as much as 75 percent to 150 percent of annual salary.

* The cost of litigation as a result of workplace violence can be a business-killer. A consultancy called The Workplace Bullying Institute estimates between turnover and lost productivity a bully could cost a Fortune 500 company up to $24,000,000; add another $1.4 million for litigation and settlement costs. A complaint that escalates to a lawsuit can easily cost hundreds of thousands of dollars and take three to five years to settle.

It's critical, as a business leader, that you work proactively to prevent and prepare for workplace violence to protect your employees and business operations. It's not only an ethical responsibility, but a bottom-line imperative.

What Can You Do About Workplace Violence?

Whether or not you and your employees intervene early in response to troubling behaviors before a potentially devastating situation escalates can make all the difference in the world in mitigating a potential loss, whether financial, emotional or physical. It's therefore essential that you create a comprehensive workplace violence prevention program at your organization if you don't already have one.

In my view, this effort needs to start in the c-suite, and should include the following strategic methodologies, all of which I cover in this book:

* **Separate the realities from the myths:** People's attitudes about workplace violence are often confused, muddled or riddled with misunderstanding and myths, which can cause real problems for the organization. Recognizing these myths and embracing the universal truths of workplace violence is the first step.

* **Enhance your leadership:** Strong and steady leadership lies at the heart of workplace violence prevention, and the leadership ethic is not just for managers. Establishing leadership principles and extending

them to every employee is a major factor in making your organization more secure and successful overall.

* **Nurture employee engagement:** A way to help prevent workplace violence is to get employees engaged. More engaged employees will lower workplace violence, and create a culture of care.

* **Encourage individual growth:** If you value a safe and secure work environment, you need to spend the time, effort and money to be sure that every employee has the very best opportunity to reach his or her full potential.

* **Make workplace violence prevention everybody's job:** Everybody in the company has a responsibility of leadership from the perspective of being observant. Educating, engaging and empowering every employee to observe and act is an essential key to your security.

* **Build the practice of ethical decision making:** When employees observe irrational behavior, they need to have the judgment to step up and say "we've got to interact; something has to be done; there's going to be some activity here."

* **Remember that what's good for the individual is good for the company:** Steps to ensure a safe workplace are good for the individual and the company. They're intertwined and critical to both safety and business success.

* **Establish strong "next practices," adapted from the guidance in this book:** Next practice development isn't about making something more efficient; instead, it is about a fundamental transformation of the core business culture to ensure that all of the moving parts of workplace violence prevention are aligned and effective.

I am often amazed at the lack of lessons learned in the realm of workplace violence. You look at Columbine, Virginia Tech and any number of other high-profile incidents, and you see a lot written on the facts of what happened, ranging from intimidation and bullying to murder, but you just don't see a lot of lessons learned.

Embracing a broad, enlightened view of the shear breadth of workplace violence, along with an understanding of the way the various levels connect, is the first step to dealing with this issue. Once you've got that foundation, you can begin to build your safe, secure organization.

GUEST EXPERT
Dealing with the Warning Signs

By Mimi Lanfranchi, *Senior Vice President, National Accounts and Specialized Services for AlliedBarton Security Services*

Concern and compassion may help a disgruntled former employee begin emotional detachment from a company and help to diminish anger. The resources involved in diffusing this and other potential workplace violence situations is a critical investment considering the possible devastating ramifications if the situation is not addressed.

As security leaders, we need to make sure that all employees understand and recognize the warning signs of workplace violence so that everyone can act as eyes and ears to report unusual behavior to security. In many cases there are warning signs for an employee who requires intervention. Experience and instinct are valuable tools for all security professionals. Any employee with one or more of the indicators represented on AlliedBarton's continuum may be in need of assistance. Managers must be alert to these indirect pleas for help and provide a positive and timely response to ensure a safe and secure work environment.

Remember that just because someone exhibits one of these behaviors does not necessarily mean they are prone to acts of violence. In fact, it rarely does. When someone has a noticeable change in behavior it is critically important to make sure that employees understand that they should consider telling a manager or someone who has authority to take action about the situation.

The behaviors we have identified are only a few of the possible warning signs of workplace violence.

The popular use of mobile technologies poses some new risks. Through threatening emails, phone texts or messages on social networking sites, workplace violence can continue, even after you have left for the day. The Internet has created new workplace harassment dangers that didn't exist a decade or so ago. According to an article in the *USA Today*, "10 percent of US employers have been subpoenaed to produce employee emails in lawsuits." One of the reasons that email and text messages play such a pivotal role in harassment cases is their immediate and seemingly informal nature.

What does this mean for security professionals? There are a growing number of lawsuits and employee complaints that include offensive text messages as evidence of the inappropriate behavior. Employers should work with their security teams to revise company policies to inform employees that harassing text messages to coworkers will be considered violations of the company's harassment policy. If an employer issues cell phones to employees, consider whether text messaging will be allowed on those phones. If text messaging is accommodated, employees using the phones need to understand that they have no right to privacy and that all text messages are subject to search and can be obtained by the employer at any time.

Social networking sites such as YouTube, Facebook and Twitter have continued to open the door for more online bullying. Any time a new method of communication is created, it's inevitable that a certain segment of employees will use that medium to convey inappropriate messages that have the potential for getting themselves—and their employers—in hot water. The problem is that monitoring these sites is virtually impossible for an employer. First, there are too many of them. Second, many sites enable users to restrict who sees their content. Third, most employers view social media as "quasi-private," and not something that should affect their employment. The same precautions should be used for these sites. Security professionals need to guide their employers in developing new social media policies.

An employee handbook or resource should offer an up-to-date workplace violence policy. Employers should educate their employees so that they clearly understand that the policy is part of their responsibility for safety. Employees should understand what to look for, be vigilant and have a means to communicate potential problems.

If something happens in your workplace, it is important for you to act immediately. First, you must focus on defusing the simmering crisis. Early de-escalation behaviors include, remaining calm, listening attentively, always treating the person with respect and dignity, isolating the situation, setting clear enforceable limits and, if necessary, using backup resources. Realize that control issues are most likely at the root of this confrontation. You may need to relocate the disruptive individual to another building or department, or in more severe cases recommend termination.

Using a mediator can be helpful, as they are neutral parties who can listen to both sides and facilitate conversation. To avoid additional disruption, it may be best to separate the parties involved, which also decreases the risk of any unnecessary confrontation.

Consider hiring a security company if you do not already have a program in place. If you currently do have security personnel, make sure that they are aware of potential workplace violence threats and prepared to take appropriate measures. An estimated 50 percent of employers report that workplace violence crimes or threats are never reported to police or security. Whether an employee is feeling physically or verbally threatened, he or she should always contact a security resource.

chapter 2

Five Myths that Could Land Your Organization in Trouble

People's attitudes about workplace violence are often confused, muddled or riddled with misunderstanding and myths. In my experience, people often have difficulty recognizing the underlying realities, and the result is that they buy into one type of denial or another. They try to pretend the risks aren't there, and take no steps to make plans, instead of taking reasonable steps to deal with situations that may arise.

I see the same myths cropping up everywhere, year after year. And in all the work we do to try to educate people about what workplace violence is, it's important that they understand that much of the "common wisdom" and everyday attitudes they encounter tend to be deceptive or just plain wrong.

Five Myths

I hear these untruths about workplace violence told in many forms, but the message is always the same. In taking a look at each of these I will point out what I consider to be the critical issues:

* **Focus:** What attitudes or misconceptions have created the myth?
* **Impact:** What's the negative impact the myth creates on our perceptions and behavior?
* **Risk:** What risk does the myth set up for your organization?

Myth 1: "It's someone else's job to prevent workplace violence"
Sometimes it can be hard to find a person who will own any part of the mission to prevent workplace violence. I find there's a lot of passing the buck. Nobody wants to get tagged with the responsibility of workplace

violence or having a line of responsibility to it—as if any one person or group of people alone could deal with it! The universal response seems to be—don't look at me, not my job!

Focus: The "not my job" syndrome is perhaps the biggest misconception. In fact, workplace violence prevention is everybody's job. This is why you see so many professionals who are trying to educate the workplace about markers—markers that you can use to detect a potential threat, even if the behavior being observed seems somewhat benign. Then the employee, no matter what his or her official job description, can pick up the phone and call somebody and say "I'm seeing some irrational behavior from this person." Yes, it's everybody's job.

Impact: The real problem here is that this attitude creates a false sense of isolation from the problem. Workplace violence has many levels and arises from a variety of factors. Everyone in the organization has to be an active observer and get engaged when situations or another employee's behavior crosses a line.

Risk: This myth ends up creating organizational apathy toward workplace violence. I think any organization that allows this kind of passive attitude in its culture is setting itself up to be vulnerable to episodes of workplace violence, simply by failing to build and reinforce cultural awareness. A strong and aware organizational culture is one of the best defenses.

Myth 2: "It can't happen here"

Among the general public and within many companies I run into this this feeling of "it can't happen here; it won't happen here; we're not that type of company." This is pretty commonplace—people often confuse the fact that something has not yet happened with the idea that it will not happen in the future. So they get complacent and operate from a false sense of security.

Focus: The main result of false security is that people sometimes ignore some of the issues or individual behaviors that can lead to a violent incident. When you get down to it, people are afraid of what could happen, they see awful things on the TV news and they don't want to believe those things could come in and disrupt their world. So they tell themselves "It can't happen here" as a kind of reassurance—but that attitude is not going to help them if a real problem shows up.

Impact: Environment and past experience do matter. Often people are completely disconnected and unobservant of people who live and work very close to them, or cross their paths daily, because they are not paying any attention at all. How many times have you heard people come out and say "I had no idea…" following a violent incident by a neighbor or coworker? Examples of this are everywhere, such as the Silver Springs intruder with the bomb strapped to his chest, the Fort Hood gunman, the Columbine and Virginia Tech shooters and others. In each instance the violent outburst was preceded by behavior that should have set off alarms and put people into action.

Risk: Every organization faces some level of risk for workplace violence —this myth represents the ultimate risk of total ignorance. Workplace violence can come from within the organization, from outside of it and from a variety of forces in play. In my long experience, the only way a strong and well-managed company can deal with this challenge is through strong and engaged leadership, thoughtful education programs and fully engaged employees—all the kinds of "next practices" that I discuss in this book.

Myth 3: "Workplace violence is usually blue-collar related."

People tend to have a bias that workplace violence is largely a blue-collar phenomenon, when actually it can happen in any job situation, anywhere. The public experiences workplace violence most commonly as extreme cases, usually a shooting or violent assault situation on the evening news, which leads to misconceptions.

Focus: Often the perpetrators in some of the most dramatic workplace violence stories that appear on the evening news are blue-collar workers who have a grudge against a boss or manager. So the media stereotype may have something to do with this perception. However, in reality any social or economic class of citizens can engage in workplace violence. To say that blue-collar workers are more likely to be involved in workplace violence creates a false perception of the wide range of individuals who are involved.

Impact: The impact here is twofold, both to put an unfair stigma on blue-collar people as perpetrators of workplace violence and to diminish awareness and attention on white-collar perpetrators and members of other social groups.

Risk: Organizations cannot afford to single out any group to be the fall guy for workplace violence. I think this myth is particularly bad for a number of reasons, the main one being that it creates a totally wrong impression. The reasons people engage in workplace violence are complex and personal and can't be boiled down to simplistic things like "blue collar" identity.

Myth 4: "Workplace violence is caused by outsiders"

Often people like to jump to the conclusion that generally it's an outsider who brings a horrible act into their workplace. I think that this may be somewhat connected to the "it can't happen here" assumption that I discussed earlier. People want to believe that any disruptive violence that comes into their space has to come from outside. It's a kind of defensive psychological reaction we can get into. It is important to deal with the larger truth that workplace violence is a web in which some elements are caused from within and some from external forces.

Focus: The outsider concept can be oddly reassuring to people who want to see the sources of danger as being entirely external. It's a way of washing their hands of the whole issue by putting it out of doors. In many ways, these attitudes are fed by the steady diet of media stories we hear about criminal activities and victimization, and the continuing drama played out on TV and the Internet where there are these constant, nameless menaces from the outside, waiting for their opportunity to strike. This makes it easy for some people to pay no attention to the potentially larger issues that may lie closer to home in their own organization.

Impact: This view doesn't face up to the fear of internal sources of workplace violence within the organization. It also doesn't address the shared responsibility of everybody in the company to help deal with it. Often, the potential sources of internal workplace violence are giving off subtle warning signs before they manifest with violent behavior. Underperforming at work, or perhaps feeling troubled and angry, they may express anger and resentment in a variety of ways on the job, or manifest early-stage violent behavior in the form of bullying and intimidating behavior. For those looking for workplace violence on the outside, they are going to miss all the indications and trouble spots in their own organization.

Risk: This position is the equivalent of an ostrich with its head in the sand. There's no way any organization can pretend that it does not face internal risks for some level of workplace violence. At the very least, each organization must understand the specific risks of exposure it faces given its lines of business, types of personnel and other risk factors. Take a look at the Roundtable features in this and other chapters for more insight related to industry particulars.

Myth 5: "It's just a matter of luck"

Really? Is that all there is to it—just dumb luck? Some people think it is. Surely there are some events that result from "luck," or more accurately, forces beyond the control of the organization, but this is not always the case. Unfortunately, some people believe that the reason they have never been touched by workplace violence comes down to their feeling that they are just lucky and bad things such as workplace violence just don't touch them at all.

Focus: People who think it's all about luck have a sense of entitlement—the bad things in the world don't touch them. The deep myth here is that just because something hasn't happened to you before doesn't mean it can't or won't happen to you tomorrow. People find it really easy to think they are invincible about some things just because they have not experienced them.

Impact: Believing that a tragic workplace violence incident may result exclusively from bad luck is just another manifestation of not understanding the causes and false complacency. This attitude may be the most dangerous myth of all, for it totally absolves you and your employees of the shared responsibility to actively prevent a tragedy. Obviously, the impact can be catastrophic.

Risk: Hiding behind the luck theory, like all these other myths, is just another way of insulating yourself from the deeper truth. Workplace violence is a real possibility in life and pretending it doesn't exist is false and dangerous. Maybe it will never touch you in your entire life. But maybe it will. And if it does, and you have taken no steps to do anything to prevent it, to mitigate it, and someone you know and care for is hurt or injured, that is something that you will carry with you.

Other Myths, Misconceptions and Points of Confusion

Beyond the "big five" myths about workplace violence I have just profiled, many smaller misconceptions shape how people understand the risks and fail to take action. Many of these additional myths and confusions are directly related to how people process media stories they see, or more accurately, how they partially process these reports and end up taking away incorrect conclusions. Other points of confusion are more deeply connected to how people create their own sense of security—often a false sense of security—and the lies they tell themselves to create that illusion. Here are two that I think are the most interesting.

"It's all about the headlines"

People think workplace violence is one big unrealistic news story that is just a set of random disconnected headlines with no rhyme or reason to it; that no matter what happens, you can never learn anything from what happens in these stories, as they are just about crazy people doing things to each other. By definition, then, people who buy into this myth think that workplace violence always happens to somebody else. In a way, it's like losing in the lottery—you drew the wrong lot!

What's really important here is that people do need to learn from these situations. When a shooter attacks a school, and if you work at a school, you need to review your own operation. What could you have done if this had happened at your school? If you're in any other kind of business, how would you have dealt with the situation of shooters on your property? Every situation is a challenge for us to look at ourselves and take responsibility for our future security.

"It only happens at the workplace"

Workplace violence can happen anywhere—just ask any employee who does field work. One of the common misconceptions people have is that incidents of workplace violence are confined to the office, factory or other formal worksite. In fact, some of the more difficult challenges for workplace violence can be field sites, where field reps must enter customer home environments secured with guard animals, and in some cases, armed individuals. Fieldwork also requires reps to enter client sites or other locations to present products, perform services or gather information.

Risk factors for fieldwork can be difficult to calculate. In most cases, field workers have a clear process of engagement to deliver customer services. In the field, however, they are alone and may be required to deal with unforeseen instances and situations, particularly when the customer, partner or individual onsite does not recognize them or reacts in a defensive or hostile manner. So it is important, once again, to prepare, manage and anticipate and help field workers be ready for unforeseen situations.

Finding Clarity

Accepting the myths about workplace violence is simply dangerous. These common misconceptions make it too easy for us not to face the truth about the evils of workplace violence, and as a result you may fail to take adequate steps leading to protection and prevention.

One of the first big challenges you face in dealing with workplace violence is getting clear on the real issues that you face in your company. The five myths I discuss here are examples of how easy it is to get lost and confused with misinformation, incorrect perceptions or oversimplifications and media generalizations. We're all susceptible at some level.

Through awareness you can begin to come to some appreciation of facts and the underlying patterns that define our understanding of workplace violence, and that can become the framework for effective leadership, attention, and action in your organization. Failure to address these very real issues can get your organization into trouble.

ROUNDTABLE
Leadership and Workplace Violence

Bill Whitmore, *Chairman & CEO, AlliedBarton Security Services*
Rich Cordivari, *Vice President, National Accounts, AlliedBarton Security Services*
Bonnie Michelman, *Director of Police and Outside Services, Massachusetts General Hospital*
Maureen Rush, *Vice President for Public Safety, University of Pennsylvania*
Chris Swecker, *former Assistant Director, Criminal Investigative Division, FBI*

Bill Whitmore: So much has been written about workplace violence, but actually there hasn't been much written about getting awareness and sponsorship at the c-suite within organizations. So that's what we're trying to do here—we're really trying to get some awareness. Related to that, how do you fight complacency, misunderstanding and that simple lack of awareness? The way that we touch customers and others who are concerned about their organizations is through seminars that we have conducted in multiple cities around the country.

Rich Cordivari: In some of the larger markets, these seminars attract no less than 150 people and in one, about 200. We ran seminars in Stamford, Connecticut twice in four months and had close to 200 people at each one. Part of the problem we're addressing in these events is the culture of denial. "It's not going to happen here if I can just ignore it."

Bonnie Michelman: There is an irony in this—complacency while at the same time people are living in fear. People are petrified of living in fear, so they get back to that complacency—the attitude of "It won't happen here."

Chris Swecker: As a security director you have your biggest challenge in getting someone interested in something that hasn't happened. If you're doing your job right, then nothing happens. So it's about creating a sense of urgency at the highest levels.

Michelman: Corporations are starting to listen now, and I think there are two reasons: one is litigation, and that gets people's attention. The other is that for most industries people have become more prudent consumers. They think about what safety in a hotel is going to be like, or if they are going to get assaulted in the parking lot of a particular big-box discount store. That will that determine who they do business with. At the same time, the obvious presence of security can unnerve a customer.

Maureen Rush: I think Bonnie just hit on an important point. You go to the hotel and you walk into room and on your pillow is a pamphlet about security. So, it's a Catch-22. In one way it's great because they care about security and then in the back of your mind you're thinking what's going on around here?

Michelman: There's a difference. If I go into a room and there are good locks, then I like that. If I saw posters that said "this is what you do if you see someone with a gun," that would scare me.

Swecker: One corporation where I advised on security was very much like this. They'd say things such as "Let's not talk about this…you are going to scare people…it doesn't happen often enough for us to be talking about it all the time…we don't want the brand to be associated with that." It's a problem.

Rush: It goes back to the point that no one effort can stand alone. Security has to be part of the bigger picture, quality of life, crisis management plan. Because everyone has an issue that they want on the forefront of the c-suite, so you have to blend it in to the return of the investment for the company or the hospital or the university.

Denial and Consequences

The five myths I focus on in this chapter are not, of course, the only misinformation that individuals and companies encounter about workplace violence. They are symptoms of what can become a "culture of denial" in some organizations. That's what happens when people, individually and in groups, refuse to face up to realities and take intelligent action based upon actual facts.

A Culture of Ignorance...or Awareness?

Some forms of workplace violence will enter from outside the working environment, such as a criminal or domestic violence situation extended into the workplace. These are situations for which the organization can make security provisions, but they do not arise directly from the company's own business culture.

Here I'd like to focus on workplace violence that arises directly from within the organization itself. On a day-to-day level, a culture of ignorance of workplace violence can lead to toleration of behaviors that may ultimately lead to manifestations of violence and, ultimately, violent events. Workplace violence is deeply embedded in human behavior patterns, and it is not all about headline news stories. Within the workplace environment, it takes the form of bullying, intimidation, and inappropriate interpersonal dialog on the job.

The problem arises when people cannot draw the distinction between business behavior that is appropriately competitive, strong, focused and directed and moments of abusive behaviors that are disrespectful, psychologically and verbally harmful—whether they actually are violent or not. I find these are very fine lines to sort out and separate. They are made even more complex by the fact that women and men tend to perceive the lines between acceptable challenge and violent intent differently (see the perceptions sidebar later in this chapter) and that is just one of the variables of perception!

Zero Tolerance

Dealing with internal workplace violence is really about building a zero-tolerance culture for bullying, intimidation and violence. The continuum graphic that appears throughout this book shows the full pattern of workplace violence, from mild to intense. It's the map for how we have to draw the line.

That's how I see the issue at my company—creating a culture where even the mild and midrange forms of workplace violence in the continuum are not acceptable. If somebody is yelling at an employee, my attitude is if you talk to our employee like that again, you're not going to work here—it's not acceptable. You need to start setting up that culture.

A culture where myths and denial about workplace violence prevails becomes one where problems can fester, in my view. And, when no lines are drawn on lower-level aggressive and intimidating behaviors, then the company is at risk for larger and more intense and potentially costly events to take place over time. It's about consequences.

Some some very distinct consequences occur when an organization fails to deal with workplace violence. The most overwhelming consequence of not appropriately dealing with the warning signs is, of course, tragic injury and loss of life to people—employees in your organization or others who are involved in an incident. Beyond any business issues, costs and liabilities that flow from such a situation, nothing else can equal its depth and finality. When that happens, there is nothing we can do to reverse the tragedy.

When management is invested in the myths—either by not directly addressing situations involving bullying or intimidation, or when directly part of the problem itself—there inevitably is going to be a loss in productivity and a negative impact on employee morale. There's no hard-and-fast rule to compute it, but organizational cultures that do not address these issues are much more vulnerable to higher employee turnover rates and staff maintenance, training and development costs as a result.

It's important to face the consequences of denial and ignorance squarely. They hit the organization's bottom line, they hit day-to-day operations, and they hurt the functional effectiveness of how the company meets its mission. But most of all they hurt people. They reduce the confidence of people in the company and the organization.

Myths that create a culture of denial can create a kind of inertia, and even worse, they can actively suppress proactive steps managers might take to deal with workplace violence. By making workplace violence seem less important or threatening, myths can have negative impact on workplace violence initiatives in a company's workplace violence programs, including:

* Failure to implement policies in place
* Failure to inform employees that polices exist
* Reluctance to discuss the topic for fear of alarming employees

Myths and misinformation that foster ignorance create a culture of denial and avoidance around workplace violence. They are negative and destructive forces to the organization. It's important for every company to be realistic about these issues, not only for the sake of its overall security, but to protect its people, property and assets. The first challenge is simply to see these common myths for what they are—dangerous misrepresentations of the risks and the threats that face every company today.

Different Perceptions

One of our larger challenges in addressing workplace violence myths is balancing perceptions between different stakeholder groups, particularly men and women. You can see the example in the following sidebar of one such example of variable perceptions between men and women, and how they interpret triggers differently. So any cultural change we create has to be a negotiated balance between these perceptions. It has to reflect the needs of different stakeholders to define what I might call a baseline of behavior for workplace violence in the organization.

Perceptions Vary on What Constitutes Workplace Violence

A clear and communicated workplace violence policy is critical for getting everyone on the same page about exactly what workplace violence is. Left on their own, workers have vastly different interpretations of it. A study by Doherty Partners LLC is one of several to show that managers feel substantially safer than line workers, and that male workers and female workers often view identical incidents differently. Some examples:

→ If a coworker has an argument with a spouse or family member at work, 77 percent of female workers perceive it as an act of workplace violence compared to 54 percent of men.

→ If a client has an outburst, 44 percent of women but only 25 percent of men see it as workplace violence.

→ If a coworker were to bring a weapon to work, 90 percent of women said they would think of it as workplace violence compared to 79 percent of men.

Although these incidents clearly have different degrees of severity, the results affirm how critical it is for an organization to educate employees on its definition of workplace violence and the range of incidents it wants employees to report.

Source: IOFM Report

From Myths to Clarity

I began this chapter with a series of common beliefs about workplace violence to illustrate how easily some people will try to avoid the truth about it. The common denominator of all these points of misinformation is that people don't want to face the fact that workplace violence can happen to or near them—as if it's always about somebody else, somewhere else or something else. It's a matter of shame to be hidden from and suppressed.

Fear like this is what prevents organizations from taking the steps to implement intelligent prevention programs. There is no particular shame —workforce violence arises from complex forces and moving parts. Some elements we can understand and manage; others we cannot. But I feel we must take every possible action in our power to raise awareness, and manage expectations on the part of our people to ensure security, knowledge and foresight to deal with these situations if they do arise.

It is essential that every organization acknowledges the risks and realities of workplace violence and face up to managing it. The way we beat this challenge is to face the hard cold truth head on.

GUEST EXPERT
Getting Proactive with Workplace Violence Prevention

By Bob Chartier, *Vice President, Business Development, AlliedBarton*

If you evaluate all the workplace violence myths in total, it tends to enforce the theory that any workforce is at risk of overlooking the potential for workplace violence, whether it involves senior level executives, mid-level employees, blue-collar workers on an assembly line, or in the proverbial "sweatshop." The work environment does not matter. If you have circumstances that agitate employees, then the potential for workplace violence increases.

The classic scenario one envisions when the topic of workplace violence surfaces is the recently terminated employee, devastated as a result with visions of his whole life abruptly ending for himself, wife and family. The news is overwhelming and emotional. The norm for many is a vision of this individual exiting the work setting, procuring some form of weapon, returning to the work environment, and deploying the weapon, injuring and possibly killing those with whom she or he worked. This is no doubt a tragic scenario, and one that has been seen all too often in the past. Lately however, society and the workforce have become increasingly aware of more subtle risk factors of workplace violence, encompassing sexual harassment, unfriendly and hostile work environments and a lack of communication among managers and employees. All of these conditions can agitate a workforce.

Adverse employment conditions, such as financial pressures and large-scale reductions in workforce, exacerbate the danger. Under these circumstances, one would be unwise to assume that workplace violence cannot happen anywhere, including in your own place of business.

For example consider a retail sales environment where the manager is constantly harping on employees for better sales figures, setting unattainable goals and then placing pressure on them to perform. The stress of this scenario, and the level of frustration that an employee may experience due to the feeling of being trapped with no relief in sight, is a common example for an enhanced workplace violence scenario.

In order to address the workplace violence threat, managers should keep in mind employee personalities and personal situations. As difficult as this may seem due to a manager's often hectic schedule, management still needs to take an aggressive posture in looking at the potential for workplace violence based upon work environment conditions. I would recommend conducting a deep dive into the work atmosphere in an effort to research avenues to improve employee morale and performance.

Additionally, many off-workplace personal issues ultimately can lead to anxiety, depression, and the threat for violence. These issues can include an untimely death in a family, an alcoholic or drug dependent family member, financial stress, and physical or mental abuse. Managers should oversee team members with these factors in mind. Without prying, stay aware of employees' personal lives and issues. Maintain relationships in which you can sincerely ask employees about their family and/or loved ones. If you observe a change in behaviors in your employees—including a lack of attention, aggression, hyper or unusually anxious, anti-social, hostility, anger, or moodiness, you should address the situation without delay.

A close personal relationship between coworkers is not always achievable. Many employees are fiercely private and will resist efforts to mix personal lives with business. There is nothing wrong or unusual with this view—in fact it is becoming more common. The message here is to use what you do know about your employees as an effective tool to improve the work environment and better manage workplace violence threats.

One of my colleagues managed an employee who was having issues with an alcoholic parent, and for about a week was exhibiting behaviors otherwise foreign to his normal jovial self. Subsequent to overhearing a rather tense phone discourse with an internal client, the manager came to the conclusion that his employee may have been under an unhealthy and potentially harmful amount of stress. At that point he decided that something needed to be done. He pulled the employee into a private office space, closed the door and asked him about his current state of mind and any concerns he may have about his work situation. The employee grew somewhat defensive, and asked to be left alone. The manager obliged, yet ten minutes later, the employee requested another private discussion, at which time a flood of emotion overwhelmed him, as he and the manager sat and discussed his daily battle with an alcoholic parent. The two chatted for about 20 minutes. Afterwards, the employee was back to his jovial self, with the understanding that he had the support of the person who managed his work environment. That meant everything to him, as it did to the manager, as the employee was a valued and productive member of the team. In total, this was about a 30-minute evolution, and a learning experience for both; potential anger diffused.

Taking the initiative is key to preventing workplace violence. We recommend that companies proactively craft a policy and procedure, and disseminate it to all employees. Train your leadership teams to understand the benefit of a healthy and productive work environment. Leaders should be able to recognize the milder forms of workplace violence and diffuse the escalation of aggression.

There is nothing wrong with an organization admitting the potential for workplace violence in the work environment. Conversely, maintaining a posture of denial will prevent your organization from recognizing the causes and achieving its potential. And, when an organization possesses a philosophy of denial, the larger community may become subject to news footage of the tragic workplace violence crime scene in an otherwise peaceful work environment.

chapter 3

Embracing the Cold Hard Truths

Much of the common perception about workplace violence stems from cultural attitudes. As I discuss in Chapter 2, those attitudes have allowed myths to take hold, making it difficult for many people to get a firm grip on a standard of truth. Once you clear the air of all the misconceptions that have grown up around workplace violence, you can begin to narrow in and face up to the facts. From those facts you can begin to really understand what this phenomenon is, and how workplace violence truly affects us.

Workplace violence statistics unfold year after year, reflecting unwanted and often tragic events in a wide range of business environments, from convenience-store robberies to industrial plants. Patterns of violent action tend to be consistent and predictable. Categories of workplace violence events are clear and defined. We know a great deal about the pattern of what happens, and how consistent these patterns are, but it's much harder to isolate why these things happen, and describe predictable and specific causes for them.

This chapter focuses upon the impact and reality of workplace violence as it is observed and experienced every day in organizations throughout the United States and beyond.

Facing the Truth

Getting to the "truth" of workplace violence involves understanding the underlying drivers that caused the events. To really understand the problem, I think it is necessary to begin with a focus on the observable realities—the events that take place, the historical pattern of activities we have built up around them, the categories we have identified and the inferences we have been able to make.

Denial and Reality

Reinforcing denial, such as "it won't happen here," often makes it easier to avoid taking critical steps to protect the company and its employees against very real dangers. At the most benign level, this might take the form of downplaying or giving a low priority to company workplace violence policies. At a more dangerous level, it might undercut efforts to implement a workplace violence policy at all, or to suppress discussion on these topics as inconvenient and uncomfortable. I am the first to agree that workplace violence is not an easy issue to raise. It clearly makes people uncomfortable. It's not light party conversation. But it is potentially a life-and-death matter. Moreover, the shockwaves and aftermath of a workplace violence event can have a profound effect on the victims and their families, as well as the culture, operations and even profitability of an organization.

The cold hard truth is exactly the opposite. Workplace violence can happen anywhere.

Even more than that, despite what people may think, workplace violence is not a function of class or ethnicity or status or lack of status. It's human nature for people to want to believe that they are somehow secure from this, but they are not.

In my experience, workplace violence arises from deep-seated forces that live within many human beings. In the right mix of circumstances, pressures and social dynamics someone may snap and a violent action or actions will take place. There simply is no magic formula that dictates who the perpetrator is, where the violent event takes place, or who will be the victims.

Seven Cold Hard Truths about Workplace Violence

The cold hard truth begins with the moment you face up to the fact that it can happen to you—right in your own office. When you accept that fundamental reality, you can begin to engage the solution.

Over the years I have tried to slice and dice this many different ways, but it always comes down to some hard, painful and fundamental truths about workplace violence events. Notice that I said events. I am not talking here about the intangible, underlying motivations and causes, the things we can't always pin down. I am focusing on the facts; the tragedies that show up in the morning newspaper, the actions that take place in the real world that we directly experience.

To boil it down and focus on the essence, here's how I see the essential core truths that define most workplace violence events.

Truth 1: It can happen anywhere

In Chapter 2 I discuss the whole range of myths that surround workplace violence, and regardless of the form and focus it takes, it all boils down to one thing. People want to pretend that workplace violence is some ugly impossible thing that by definition happens someplace else, that can't enter their secure world.

Despite the many wishful myths and denial, nobody is safe from random workplace violence. It can truly happen anywhere. The perpetrator might be a disaffected employee, an activist true believer, an aggravated spouse of one of the company's workers or a criminal on the premises. Workplace situations arise from dynamic circumstances that we can categorize and in some cases forecast. So every organization has to get smart and build effective awareness for the possibility that these events can possibly take place.

Truth 2: It can happen to anyone

The greatest single challenge to the "truth" is the central myth that anyone is somehow magically immune. One thing most people want desperately to believe about workplace violence is that "it can't happen to me."

Part of this is psychologically grounded in deep and habitual ways of thinking. When we have never actually experienced a radical situation like workplace violence, it is a simple psychological step of denial for us to believe we never will. In his bestselling book, *The Black Swan*, Nassim Nicholas Taleb calls these explosive, rare and radical events, such as 9/11, "Black Swan" events, and explains in detail how we simply can't accept that such things could ever happen to us, even if the possibility is raised and explained as a hypothesis. Deep in our minds, a secure area says, "Because it hasn't happened yet, it never will," and we hold on to this, almost like a security blanket.

The truth, of course, is that workplace violence can happen anywhere and it can happen to anybody. Workplace violence is not logical, nor does it respect the rights of the innocent. Whatever motivations have engaged the perpetrator, once the event has taken off, whoever happens to be close at hand is at risk regardless of whether they are involved with the perpetrator or not. Innocent people are often grievously injured or killed in these events.

Another dimension of "it can't happen to me" comes from social reinforcement. To the extent that workplace violence becomes a socially visible and engaged topic, denial then becomes "it can't happen to us." I have experienced this sort of social interaction in many forms as part of overall security planning. While the focus of security is to anticipate threats that might arise internally and from the outside, I have observed situations where the planning teams feel that internally generated workplace violence is not possible. As for externally generated workplace violence, often there seems to be a misplaced confidence that the quality of their planning may be sufficient to ward off any such occurrence.

People don't know how to understand these heartbreaking experiences. These stories are often so enormous and emotionally overwhelming that people can't really assimilate them. Perhaps they think the victim wasn't thoroughly prepared, or that the character of people involved was different than theirs, or that the dynamics of the situation was utterly different than the higher qualities of their own organization. When I listen to some people talk about how this "can't happen to us," I hear a dangerous culture of denial taking form.

Again, there are many people in organizational life who harbor a false sense of security and believe they are somehow immune, but such thinking only puts them more at risk. Why? Because it deters them from taking effective action to anticipate and build policies to cope.

Truth 3: There may be advance indications

Although warning signs may help us anticipate when a situation may take shape and erupt into violence, we cannot forecast a workplace violence event with complete certainty (I discuss the challenges of discerning these warning signs in Chapter 1). Nor can we always identify someone who may erupt with a violent act. Still, certain patterns of behavior may forecast a violent event. For example, it certainly is true that many workplace violence events take place in association with employee terminations, and the enraged employee seeks to take revenge on the manager, supervisor or others at the company.

Although in some cases people commit horrible acts of violence with no prior indication whatsoever, in other instances an individual moving toward such an act sometimes will display changes in typical behavior. This may take

Workplace Violence Continuum

AlliedBarton's Workplace Violence Continuum

the form of consistent belligerence toward coworkers, changes in appearance, increased talk of weapons, random hostility in interpersonal communications, or any number of other behaviors as indicated in the continuum.

In some cases, the perpetrator is known as a virulent, threatening person, is preoccupied with weapons or may have a well-known obsession with shootings. All these traits, individually and collectively, are indications that an individual may have violent tendencies, but none of them represents a "smoking gun" that the individual is ready to commit an act of workplace violence in the future.

Truth 4: Financial motivations are often involved

I am the first to admit that we don't fully understand all the motivations that drive a perpetrator to commit an act of workplace violence. But I am very clear that the most extreme events are often driven by a financial situation.

The classic workplace violence cliché, often called "going postal," involves the terminated employee facing loss of income who takes violent revenge upon the company. The object of these acts is usually the manager who did the firing or some other authority, but the anger driving the behavior is the desperation of the individual without a job who fears he or she has no prospects. Underlying acts are the financial power and influence of the organiza-tion, which provide key points of motivation—the "little guy against the big guy" syndrome.

Truth 5: Brand damage is an inevitable consequence

Though it does not compare to the potential human toll, the organization certainly is a victim in the aftermath of an episode of workplace violence. In the event of a full-scale workplace violence incident involving an assault on company property that involves injury and death, the organization becomes fully engaged in the aftermath of the episode. Beyond dealing with the tragedy of those who are injured and possibly killed in the attack, the organization must cope with the damage to its reputation and brand. News coverage follows, and in the glare of scrutiny, the company and its executives are expected to show extraordinary sensitivity to how they manage the human victims, and the survivor's plight.

A workplace violence incident may open up unexpected lines of sight to aspects of the corporate culture that do not hold up well in the glare of media coverage. Public attention may turn to areas where the organization is weak. Brand damage may flow either from perceptions that conditions at the company are negatives, revealed by the perpetrator incident, or from percep-tions that the company has negatively managed the aftermath of the incident.

Truth 6: Long-term emotional damage continues in the aftermath

Workplace violence affects individuals and organizations long after the physical threat has abated. The organization has to play a role in helping people to recover from them, beginning with psychological first aid at the scene of the incident (something I cover in Chapter 8). Long-term emo-tional damage is an absolute consequence of these events. Those who were present for the event may have witnessed life-altering scenes and experi-ences. They may require some form of therapy and ongoing support from the organization and the community well past the point when the after-math has settled and the primary issues of the event have been dealt with.

There also may be connected issues related to injured or deceased employee families and dependents. The formal requirements and obligations the company has to its people are one thing. However, the larger issue here is being seen as coping with the extended aftermath of an extraordinary situa-tion in a strong and effective way through leadership and engagement.

The emotional damage of workplace violence is profound. Your organization must understand its role in helping to address it from all perspectives, ranging from those of the people immediately affected to the larger circle of business stakeholders and customers.

Truth 7: Most victims of workplace violence events are women

Finally, perhaps, the ugliest truth of them all: As much as it pains me to say this, when I look at the full spectrum of workplace violence—from the most basic office bullying and intimidation to more aggressive physical abuses all the way up to violent physical injury and assault—the majority of the victims are women.

Facing up to the cold hard truths about workplace violence against women means to understand how violence works across the business spectrum in all forms of physical and verbal intimidation. In some situations violence can escalate to actual physical contact in conflict situations. In scenarios where strength brings advantage, women often are at a disadvantage.

Our own nationwide survey found that 33 percent of women working outside the home report being personally affected by workplace violence. This compares to 24 percent of men reporting this impact. We found that open hostility is the most common form of workplace violence affecting women personally, with about one in four (23 percent) of women personally affected, as compared to 16 percent of men. Bullying and harassment is also more likely to affect women than to affect men, with 17 percent of women reporting these incidents.

With nurses, a profession that employs many females, it's worse. They experience workplace violence at a rate 72 percent higher than medical technicians, and at more than twice the rate of other medical fieldworkers, according to the National Crime Victimization Survey.

Profiles and Causes

It's important to remember that the point of instigation for workplace violence can be from outside of a company or within, whether from a criminal, customer or client, coworker, a spillover of a domestic situation or a terrorist/true believer. A single perpetrator is often the starting point for a workplace violence incident, but situations can arise from more complicated family and social scenarios in which the perpetrator is deeply engaged. In these cases there may be a superficially visible tipping point that leads to violence—a fight with a supervisor, a spouse, a crime gone wrong—but inevitably that single instance is just the tip of an iceberg. It's often a single violent expression stemming from a range of personal troubles.

Recognizing these common causes can help make some sense of actual workplace violence events, particularly those attacks leading to death and serious injury that make up police blotter caseloads. These tend to draw the greatest levels of attention and scrutiny simply because of the level of shock and trauma they cause. Any attempt to profile the possible causes is admittedly a generalization that will leave some outliers and square pegs, but some broad patterns do emerge, including the following:

- **Lifestyle issues:** Often a male who is dissatisfied with his current situation, maybe as the result of divorce or other life change.

- **Job performance issues:** Lack of advancement or outright failure at career goals.

- **Behavior toward others:** Socially maladjusted and either withdrawn or frequently negative and bitter, with few friends or positive personal relationships.

- **Perceived work issues:** May have negative perceptions at work centered upon lack of advancement.

- **Personal dissatisfaction; grievances:** May blame lack of advancement upon one or more specific individuals; supervisor and/or manager are often highly likely.

- **Customer or client relationships:** Attitudes toward supervisors and managers carry over to any interactions with customer or clients.

- **Religious beliefs:** Extremely rigid, passionately held religious beliefs sometimes drive individuals to violence.

The Risks of Perpetrator Profiling

I can relate many common perpetrator profiles from my work with workplace violence over the years. There is much we know in the security industry about the people who commit these acts and inflict this violence. I also know it is very important to be careful about casually putting individuals into a box.

As I've discussed, most workplace violence is not the headline news variety. It's the everyday stuff you never see—milder and midrange behavior as is shown in the continuum. The perpetrators of lower-level intimidation are not necessarily going to have the same profile as the people who would engage in extreme violence, but they could have. This is an inexact science at one level. We have to be attentive to the realities we have observed and learn from what we have experienced.

The problem with profiling is that it makes things a little too easy and too stereotypical. The following, for example, is a typical police department-style profile of a workplace violence perpetrator who is an internal employee of an organization. It is essentially a portrait of the classic "going postal" guy who has a very loose hold on his job and is about to get fired for lousy performance:

+ Male

+ 35 years or older

+ A history of violence towards women, children and/or animals

+ An unstable work history

+ Loner with little or no family or social support

+ Tends to externalize blame for things gone wrong

+ Accepts criticism poorly

+ Medium to heavy use of drugs or alcohol

+ Possible military history

+ Owns firearms or other dangerous weapons

In my experience, workplace violence perpetrators are a lot more complex than this. We have to look at a wider range of people and experiences to fully understand the phenomenon. This profile accounts for only one of the five categories of identified perpetrators, after all.

My point is simply this: the classic "employee shooter" scenario is just one case in a much broader tapestry. To really understand workplace violence and the nature of where the perpetrator comes from, the cold hard truth is that we have to reach beyond that convenient cliché.

As I discuss in Chapter 1, while every situation and set of circumstances is unique, some warning signs are commonly exhibited by individuals in need of assistance. These include a full range of indications, ranging from unusual tardiness and work absences to accelerated abuse of drugs and alcohol and visible obsession with or talk about weapons. Warning signs vary in some details from person to person, but whatever form they take, they could reflect anger, alienation and a personal desire for revenge against real or imagined wrongs.

Truths for Government and Public Services

The truths of workplace violence are pretty universal. That said, the federal, state and local government sectors have unique circumstances that can require a special understanding to fully understand the risks they face. The potential for violence in this sector may vary significantly among individual operational institutions within the government as a whole.

Typical Workplace Facilities

As we all know, governmental entities operate a variety of public service offices. Some of the most visible and common are institutions such as the U.S. Postal Service or state offices such as the Department of Motor Vehicles (DMV). The U.S. government commonly operates large federal building sites where a variety of agencies are grouped, often including passport offices and various forms of business licensing and other specialized government services.

These facilities have special risks, as we've witnessed all too well. In the wake of the April 19, 1995 domestic terrorist attack on the Federal Building in Oklahoma City, and the September 11, 2001 destruction of the World Trade Center by international terrorists, the federal government has adopted a significantly more aggressive approach to security. Larger government facilities have been progressively hardened and secured due to higher perception of risks for externally generated violence from domestic or international terrorist groups.

Risks and Incidents

On a different level, the government employs so many people and offers so many services at such a level of open access that it is inherently vulnerable to random incidents of violence such as the famous "going postal" incidents widely reported in the press. Here are a few examples:

* **Going Postal:** On August 19, 1983, a former United States Postal Service employee returned to his workplace in Johnston, South Carolina with a shotgun and a grudge. He killed the postmaster and wounded two others. Since then, the "going postal" scenario has played

out with deadly consequences in dozens of cities and has come to symbolize acts of anger and extreme violence in the workplace. Although the term entered the security industry vocabulary associated with disaffected mail carriers, there is no job category delineation that allows assumptions of safety to be made based on titles or types of facilities.

* **City Council Attack:** In February 2008, a disgruntled St. Louis area contractor, angered that he had not secured construction work from a municipal project, went on a shooting rampage during a public city council meeting, killing six and injuring two.

* **Courthouse Assault:** In January 2010, after failing to prevail with a social security claim, a man walked into a Las Vegas Federal Courthouse lobby and opened fire. The shooting lasted for several minutes, claiming the life of a security officer and ending only after the shooter was shot and killed. The gunman could have killed many more people had the armed security officer and a deputy marshal not been present at the courthouse.

Other nongovernmental or regulated public facilities and agencies such as utilities also affect this sector, as deregulation can cause dramatic economic impacts on individual rate-payers, leading to double-digit percentage increases for essential gas, electric, water or sewer services. This may attract large numbers of angry citizens to public meetings.

The safety of public officials has become a higher priority in recent years. Most municipalities, counties, state agencies and federal facilities are supported by integrated security and law enforcement programs, but elected officials are clearly not the only subjects of workplace violence.

While robust access control and screening may protect designated government facilities, companion buildings in many complexes house significant numbers of agencies or bureaus that may be totally open and uncontrolled. The risk to the public worker is compounded when the potential of violence from public interaction with government employees is combined with potential domestic violence that could follow a government employee to the office.

Recessionary pressures coupled with a high unemployment rate and rising costs of living create a climate where emotions and personal tragedies could set the stage for more violent government workplace scenarios. The easy victims may be the accessible bureaucrat, removed from the political process. Although merely the facilitator of policy, that person still represents a soft target for expressions of extreme frustration and anger.

Truths for Education

Education is one of the largest industries in the United States when taken as a whole, encompassing K-12 public schools, private schools and higher education from junior colleges all the way up to university-level institutions. The campus environment is where the majority of institutionalized education processes takes place, even allowing for the current evolution to online and Internet-based university programs.

Typical Workplace Facilities

Education workplace facilities may range from K-12 school sites to university campuses. The basic school site is comprised of classroom clusters, play yard, and usually a cafeteria or eating space and some specialty education rooms and a library. A full-scale university is a city in miniature, with complete structures devoted to class and education purposes, dormitories, scientific research labs, libraries, theaters, medical facilities and hospitals.

Educational institutions typically value an open and accessible style and culture as a part of their mission. So campus environments typically allow a free flow of people in and out of the facility.

Risks and Incidents

The classic education violence situation that has defined itself in the news is the disaffected active shooter who goes on a rampage against fellow students and faculty within the campus environment. Such shooters have been able to wreak substantial damage and death before they have been overpowered and subdued or have taken their own lives.

We are all familiar with the most notable examples of violence in education:

- The Virginia Tech massacre was a school shooting that took place on April 16, 2007, on the campus of Virginia Polytechnic Institute and State University in Blacksburg, Virginia. In two separate attacks, approximately two hours apart, the perpetrator, Seung-Hui Cho, killed 32 people and wounded many others before committing suicide. The massacre is the deadliest shooting incident by a single gunman in U.S. history.

→ The Columbine High School massacre occurred on Tuesday, April 20, 1999, at Columbine High School in Columbine, an unincorporated area of Jefferson County, Colorado, near Denver and Littleton. Two seniors at the school, Eric Harris and Dylan Klebold, embarked on a massacre, killing 12 students and one teacher. They also injured 21 other students directly, and three people were injured while attempting to escape. The pair then committed suicide. It is the fourth-deadliest school massacre in United States history, after the 1927 Bath School disaster, 2007 Virginia Tech massacre and the 1966 University of Texas massacre, and the deadliest for an American high school.

Violence in education is a day-to-day proposition beyond these dramatic, isolated incidents of gun violence. Campus security must manage and deal with situations involving physical intimidation, assault, beatings of both male and female students, and sexual harassment cases as well. Student dormitories can often prove to be the scene of violent incidents, threats and assaults. The campus represents a full range of challenges for violent interactions.

Truths for the Petrochemical Industry

The U.S. petrochemical industry includes the oil and gas and chemical processing businesses. These companies maintain operations to extract key natural resources and to process and refine them into usable substances for sale on U.S. and international markets. These are highly complex businesses that often involve work with highly toxic, dangerous substances and demand high levels of organizational responsiveness and effectiveness.

Typical Workplace Facilities

Petrochemical companies maintain business offices around the U.S., with many of their operations headquartered in or around Houston. The core of their functional operations are in refineries, chemical processing plants, or in other resource-gathering operations that they operate.

Risks and Incidents

Refineries and chemical plants have been identified as likely terrorist targets by the Department of Homeland Security, particularly since the 9/11 attacks. Refineries sited in urban areas could explode into a massive wide ranging, escalating catastrophe.

Chemical plants represent a different risk altogether. Depending upon the nature and toxicity of chemical substances employed at a given plant, an attack upon the plant could release hazardous materials into the air and cause potentially lethal release of toxins over a wide area. Any act of one-one-one workplace violence in this type of facility could create significant second-tier consequences of chemical release or explosion beyond the initial attack.

Currently, some U.S. states are creating new laws that allow concealed weapons on these sites. While workers would not be permitted to carry weapons into the office, guns could be present in personal vehicles parked on the property. There generally are no exceptions in these laws for highly volatile and exceptional facilities such as refineries or chemical processing plants with extremely high security requirements.

Truths for Healthcare

The Healthcare industry touches every American in some way every year. The industry is massive and reaches into every corner of our national life. The focal points for an understanding of workplace violence are the large institutions that increasingly are coming to dominate the delivery of care and services to the great mass of American citizens. Due to the unique scope and potential workplace violence profile for this sector, I've dedicated Chapter 10 of this book to this topic.

Typical Workplace Facilities

Within the large healthcare concern, there are medical offices where patients meet their doctors, and hospitals where large-scale inpatient and outpatient services are provided.

Large medical plan hospitals are often where all services are provided—they are where the system has aggregated all the latest equipment, medical talent and tools.

The most volatile area in the hospital is the emergency room, where dramatic life-and-death, cases come in the front door. In inner-city areas, the ER will often get gunshot cases following gang violence episodes, with friends and family members of the wounded following them into the facility.

Pharmacies are also key areas of interest, in that drugs are often a target for criminal activity and violence. In particular, drug addicts seeking highly addictive substances such as OxyContin have been known to perform desperate break-and-enter operations to smash secured areas in pharmacy and physician offices and commit other violent crimes to obtain the object of their addiction.

Addiction and its consequences in general form a critical focus and motivation that represents a risk factor for workplace violence in healthcare. Individuals who are addicted to one drug or another have demonstrated repeatedly that they will engage in extreme behaviors right up to the edge of life and death—and put medical staff at risk.

Risks and Incidents

More than 60 percent of all nonfatal workplace assaults occur in hospitals, nursing homes, residential care facilities, and other social-service locations, making this a hot-button sector for security and prevention. Some of the more dramatic examples of violence include the following:

* **Emergency Room Assaults:** *The Journal of Nursing Administration* published a study in the July/August 2009 issue titled "Violence Against Nurses Working the U.S. Emergency Departments" which demonstrated that violence against emergency department (ED) nurses is highly prevalent. Twenty-five percent of survey respondents reported experiencing physical violence more than 20 times in the past three years and other studies have found that 30 to 80 percent of hospital staff has been physically assaulted at least once during their careers.

* **Drug-Induced Violence:** *Workplace Violence News* reported a classic incident years ago involving an ambulance-borne patient and a deputy sheriff at an emergency department entrance. The patient was in an apparent stupor and could not be easily revived. As the medical staff attempted to draw blood with an IV, the patient suddenly and violently exploded in a mindless rage—needle, syringe and blood flying. The deputy attempted to restrain him, as did attending nurses and police, resulting in injuries all around. Three officers arrived from the station, and it took all of them plus the deputy sheriff to cram the subject into the squad car. As it turns out, the patient was on PCP, or angel dust, which resulted in his bizarre and dangerous behavior.

ROUNDTABLE
Violence in Public Institutions

Bill Whitmore, *Chairman & CEO, AlliedBarton Security Services*
Chris Swecker, *former Assistant Director Criminal Investigative Division, FBI*
Bonnie Michelman, *Director of Police and Outside Services, Mass General*
Maureen Rush, *Vice President for Public Safety, University of Pennsylvania*

Bill Whitmore: Campus violence is prevalent. I just saw it with one of my sons at his college. One of his roommates in college was taken away from campus and never came back. Something happened off campus. I don't know what it was, my son doesn't even know, but it was because of some violent act that probably had a drug connection. These issues are out there and I don't think we talk about them enough.

Maureen Rush: Urban colleges make the security situation even more complex. Our campus is spread throughout the city streets. So if some shady and potentially violent character is coming our way, and if he walks down Walnut Street, my police officer may investigate him for being on campus. But it's really not on campus—it's a city street, even though we have academic buildings right there. So it's going to be shades of gray here. It's going to be hard to keep him out of the environment.

Chris Swecker: That Virginia Tech message was undeniably clear. If on-campus violence didn't have everyone's attention before, it certainly has their intention now.

Rush: Government oversight brought on by tragedy has forced universities to embrace workplace violence prevention. A case in point is Jeanne Clery, who was murdered in her dorm room 26 years ago at what was considered a "sleepy" university. Jeanne's mother told me that they had a choice between Tulane or this place, and they thought that Tulane had too much violence. And inside of her dorm room, she gets raped, tortured and murdered by a fellow student who had access to the dormitory, not her room. So from that the federal government has stepped in and has pressured the universities into compliance through the Clery Act.

Michelman: In my sector there's complacency about workplace violence prevention that belies the fact that we have 25,000 threats each year. When you have a shooting, and I've had it at my place, people freak for a while, they overreact for a time, and then the attitude goes back to that complacency. They have to realize that the threat is there all the time.

Rush: Universities have a lot of federal mandates for timely notification, and they're being fined for not following them. In the university markets we've been able to do more proactive work because unlike corporate America, the people who are making that organization run are parents paying tuition. And at the end of the day, what's most important to those people, aside from the good academic experience for those kids, is bringing each kid home alive. I don't know any organization that does not have a crisis management plan, and in every case a workplace violence prevention program should be folded into it.

The Honesty Factor

How we view workplace violence, and how we cope with it, brings us to a deeper understanding of human nature. Episodes of violence represent human beings at their extremes—moments when a person is at the end of the emotional highway and has nowhere to go. Something snaps, and life and death hang in the balance.

But is it possible that every human being could possibly be capable of criminal behavior at some time under certain circumstances? It's that old idea that's been around for years that "everybody in society has their price" in a risk/reward calculation. Freely translated, what that means is that most people, no matter who they are, might do something criminal if the money or the motivation were big enough.

The "Honesty Arc" shown in the following graph provides an example. It breaks down the population into two extremes of five percent. One of these represents the person who is completely honest that will never perform a criminal act under any circumstance—100 percent integrity. The other, of course, is its opposite, a complete retrograde criminal element that will lie, cheat, and steal at any opportunity. The remaining 90 percent—which I believe includes most of us—are people who under some circumstance just might slip off the edge of perfection and commit some kind of crime.

Here's a very basic example: I admit that I speed at times when I believe that police presence may be absent. Well, you may say, "Speeding isn't really a crime!" But it's breaking the law! And it is one step toward other levels of breaking the law...going even faster.

The next question the Honesty Arc would bring to bear is "Under what circumstances would the 90 percent find themselves able and willing to

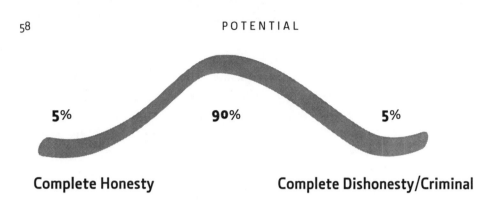

5%   90%   5%

Complete Honesty   Complete Dishonesty/Criminal

All people in society have their price or turning point in a risk/reward calculation.

commit a violent act?" It's a challenge and a deep question. Most of the 90 percent are just like you and me—law-abiding citizens who want to do the right thing. But there are special situations and pressures that can happen to people who have all these impulses that have pushed them over the edge.

So the Honesty Arc suggests there must be some profile of a person who absolutely would not create a violent act. And there must be another profile for a person who is almost certain to commit violence. For the other 90 percent there may be a potential to commit a violent act on the spur of the moment in response to pressures or temptation under certain specific circumstances.

From a law enforcement perspective, the upper five percent who would not commit a violent act are not a problem. The bottom five percent are disposed to commit criminal acts. For the remaining 90 percent, the challenge is to raise the bar through prevention and obstacles—to make the consequences so threatening and forbidding that they will be able to counteract any pressures a typical person may face to commit a violent act when they are under stress.

We need to balance the inherent honesty within people with the real stresses they face in the world. The cold hard truth is that life produces many unforeseen challenges that are often beyond an individual's ability to handle. Balancing honesty with consequences is how we must contain the urge to commit violence.

Dealing with Cold Hard Truth

When people stop pretending that it can't happen here and it can't happen to them, they have to face the real potential for workplace violence. When you really see the consequences of these cases—for example, a deranged person gone on a gun rampage and innocent people lying dead, their families stunned and grieving—you can begin to understand why the truth is important.

The truth matters because it is the first step in making a difference. The more we know about these cases, the more we can infer and build knowledge about what causes them. The more we collect that knowledge, then the greater our ability to affect a security response, to anticipate and structure our approach to workplace violence, to make a difference.

Above all else, it is important to be focused on learning the truth about workplace violence, as unpleasant and painful as it is. It's too easy to avert our eyes and try to pretend it's not there, but doing that only makes our collective problem worse. The more we really take steps to see what is happening, and get to the bottom of problems, the better our chance to find a true solution.

GUEST EXPERT
Workplace Violence in the Government Services Sector

By Charles Bohnenberger, *Vice President of Government Services, AlliedBarton*

Workplace violence happens in private and public enterprises alike. When it occurs in the government sector it often triggers more intensive media coverage and the causes may not be associated with revenge-seeking coworkers or vindictive spouses.

During the last two decades, courthouses and government buildings have been hardened against threats, while companion buildings in many capitals or complexes that house significant numbers of agencies or bureaus may be totally open and uncontrolled. The risk to the public worker is compounded when the potential of violence from public interaction with government employees is combined with potential domestic violence that could follow a government employee to the office.

Making sure that risk potential is a mainstream component of an effective threat assessment process can lead to the development of a realistic and effective security program.

Begin by conducting a thorough survey that considers a broad base of data including community crime rates, the potential of violent behavior within employee and visitor populations and the attractiveness of the facility as a target. Use assessment questions that drill into details that challenge how business is conducted. Are criminal background checks required for contractors given access to the facility? Are there robust and consistent access control procedures that don't make exceptions for staff? What packages are scanned, and are "free passes" part of your culture? This helps focus on policies and procedures that could reduce future risks and can be very wide-ranging, encompassing human capital practices, physical security processes and guidelines for interaction with the public.

Sometimes recommendations clash with organizational cultures and trade-offs may be made that result in compromises that may run counter to industry recommendations or best practices. Most security managers agree that the objective is to implement an effective security process while preserving the environment that supports productivity. Balancing resources between public policing and private security is often a critical part of a total security solution that focuses on workplace violence prevention by providing different layers of protection around and in a facility.

In many jurisdictions, especially among cash-strapped state and municipal organizations, budgets directly affect where, when or how much law enforcement can be used to control access or perimeters. The capital police in Harrisburg, Pennsylvania, for example, are tasked with perimeter control of government buildings but do not have enough staff to patrol inside. Outsourcing with contract security companies has become a cost-saving option for several Pennsylvania agencies who want to ensure that police are on point and nearby for traditional law enforcement duties, while access control patrols with armed or unarmed security officers add depth to the security program and stay within budget.

Luckily, the vast majority of the public comes to government facilities for legitimate reasons and with good intentions. Security efforts are judged, usually in hindsight, by the ability to interdict the one-percent or less that looks at government, its workers and its facilities through a jaundiced agenda. We know that the realities of violence surround us. We have a duty to work together to ensure that government remains a safe haven for the work that supports our communities and lives. There is a place for private security in the government space. We have a collaborative mandate to build working relationships with our public partners that respect and leverage mutual strengths as we keep our eyes on the safety and security prize.

chapter 4

Establishing Next Practices for Your Organization

A tragic murder-suicide took place in September 2011 at a home improvement store in Concord, North Carolina. A 25-year-old woman was working as a cashier when her angry husband came through the entrance just after 5 p.m. Apparently the couple had been in an argument. In a classic case of domestic violence spillover, the husband drew a gun and shot his wife, then turned the weapon on himself near the registers at the front of the facility. According to news reports, the couple had three children.

Incidents such as this certainly call for increased vigilance, driven from the top down, as well as constant, creative re-examination of the security policies that any company or property may already have in place. We learn new sensitivities from each episode that we can use to improve how we react in the future. People like me, with lifelong careers in law enforcement and physical security, tend to see patterns emerging from different types of workplace violence events. These must be examined with a good dose of "thinking outside of the box" to anticipate the unthinkable.

Dealing with workplace violence must begin with a systematic attempt to understand our reactions to it while preventing reoccurrence in the future. Most major organizations use the expression "best practices" to describe high performance techniques that help them make more money or accelerate time-to-market product delivery.

Best practices serve industry well. They are based on proven results, a success story, an established technique—something grounded in known factors we have already experienced. Workplace violence, however, is a continually reshaping and dynamic set of experiences, and people's lives are on the line. Even within known and familiar formats of violent action, incidents such as the Virginia Tech shootings brought new and unanticipated angles to the actual events.

In my view, standard best practices in the service of workplace violence prevention can be enhanced to be even more effective. We need ways to stretch our thinking and anticipate future events not yet seen, so in this chapter I discuss future planning and strategic thinking through an enhanced approach that increasingly is being called next practices.

An Enhanced Way of Looking at Issues

Depending on the organization, the meaning and quality level of best practices can vary widely. In some organizations, best practices may represent some very highly developed business process that is shared systematically. For example, I have experienced best practice cultures in finance and HR departments, as well as in professional organizations, which make a point of sharing effective business techniques.

Best practices often are tactical solutions implemented by line managers in the course of day-to-day business, and these can be useful in managing and helping to build a zero-tolerance culture for workplace violence—particularly when paired with our workplace violence continuum tool. However, leaders who are managing the workplace violence challenges of the future need something more than just the answers we have captured from the past. In this sense, there are no "best practices" for c-suite security executives who live day-to-day on the front lines of risk and the unknowns. To help these executives see beyond our current level of knowledge, we need an enhanced way of looking at the challenges.

Defining Next Practices

There is a growing movement in management to develop new approaches to business challenges through creative thinking that takes the form of *next* practices. Where best practices enable you to do what you are currently doing in the context of what has worked in the past, next practices can increase your organization's potential to accomplish what it could never have done before.

Even the most forward-thinking executives often have to battle the tendency to stay settled comfortably in the comfort of status-quo thinking. Most of us are grounded in our business worldview of the here and now, the present day and our experience of the past. This worldview acts like a set of blinders, if you will. It keeps us trapped in a narrow mindset of what has worked in the past, and prevents us from seeing the future in a fresh light, or from different points of view.

The first element in building next practices is to challenge status quo assumptions. There are a variety of methods and techniques to do this, some of which I discuss later in this chapter and throughout this book. Next practices can take the form of simple brainstorming, looking at business processes and situations and breaking them down to the moving parts to build newer and smarter processes. It can be drawing ideas, models and inspiration from other businesses and applying them to your own.

The bottom line is that next practices in your organization are strategic solutions that enable you to better anticipate and respond to workplace violence situations. They will help you build on your experience to date, help you recognize risk situations for violence, anticipate these situations before they mature into something threatening or worse, and manage them more effectively.

 Next Practices Insight

Q & A with Scott Hamilton, *Executive Director, Executive Next Practices Institute, Los Angeles, California*

Scott Hamilton also is the Co-founder and Senior Partner of Allign, a company that serves global Fortune 500 through midmarket companies to align and focus the entire workforce into unified, accelerated and measurable action.

Q: *What are the challenges that next practices help us to address?*
Hamilton: What we have woken up to through the recent recession—both leaders and organizations get stuck in past patterns of thinking. Legacy patterns of thinking behavior and operating prevent leaders from meeting today's economic operating and workforce challenges, and getting beyond the status quo.

Q: *How do you define or describe what next practices are?*
Hamilton: Next practices really include looking at polices,

practices, behavior and techniques that will exponentially take us forward as organizations and leaders. At the same time next practices must have a measurable component to them so they can provide a return on investment north of five, 10, 20, or even 100 percent to our organizations.

Q: *What do you feel makes next-practice thinking effective for senior executives?*

Hamilton: Next-practice thinking requires a cross-functional focus so that you are not looking at it alone. You need to have many people looking at an issue together. Not only the CEO, but the CMO, the CFO, the HR director. They can then examine any issue in a holistic way. The organization is looking at it from a common framework—the next practice function comes from the diversity of ideas and collaborations around those ideas.

Identifying Your Risks and Opportunities

One of the easy ways to get started framing next practices for workplace violence prevention is to identify the key issues facing your organization using analysis tools that are commonly familiar to most businesses. These tools help to break down various situations and scenarios so that you can more clearly see the individual parts that make up your workplace dynamics. At that point you can start a new approach to thinking about both the existing risks as well as effective solutions for addressing them.

SWOT: Strengths Weaknesses Opportunities Threats

SWOT analysis is a strategic planning method used to evaluate the strengths, weaknesses, opportunities and threats in our policy or planning assumptions. By focusing on a workplace violence prevention project objective, this method can be used to help brainstorm the key defining factors that are favorable or unfavorable to achieve that objective. A SWOT for a workplace violence prevention project would be focused around information targets like these:

 ✦ **Strengths:** Characteristics of the workplace violence prevention policy or project that will likely drive success.

❖ **Weaknesses:** Areas of the project that need work or additional development.

❖ **Opportunities:** Support from internal or external groups that will aid the project's success.

❖ **Threats:** External elements in the environment that could cause trouble for the project.

A holistic tool such as a SWOT analysis can help you get all the cards on the table. You may choose to focus on leveraging opportunities as the leading edge of your effort, or to address and minimize weaknesses and threats. In whatever case, the information you gain is the starting point of your strategic logic.

Risk Analysis

Risk analysis is another time-honored technique used to identify factors that may complicate or inhibit success in reaching a goal. Reduced to its essence, a risk analysis entails making a list of everything that could go wrong in a given worksite situation and coming up with your best response on how to deal best with each scenario.

When you are looking at your workplace violence policy and planning considerations, risks abound. You need to assess different levels of risk based on the level of potential violence and exposure to danger in a situation, and the urgency of response required. I have found that just engaging in the activity of thinking through a risk exercise tends to open up new perspectives on where the risks are and what potential responses might be.

For example, consider this sampling of the unique risks present in various business sectors:

❖ **Public Facilities:** The more public the facility, generally the more prone it is to workplace violence, and if you add an emotional factor the risks increase further. A prime example of this is healthcare, where workplace violence seems to be an increasingly larger and more critical issue, and that is why I've dedicated a special chapter to it in this book. Higher education also is a hot spot, and you can assume that workplace violence risks are going to be a whole lot higher at public places such as the parking authority offices of a large city where people pay their tickets.

- ➤ **Worksite Risks:** What about worksites that are prone to violence, such as a check-cashing agency or a convenience store? There are also additional special considerations in retail, such as the case of the big-box discounter where 160 incidents occurred in the parking lot, while incidents in the store were rare.

- ➤ **Building Access:** Many office buildings are still very permeable, though much less so since 9/11. These buildings often are open to the public, with multiple occupants representing a broad segments of society. These venues often resist staged access control procedures due to business issues.

The lesson here? You're more exposed in certain environments than others, with unique considerations and solutions required for protecting each of them.

Next Practices for Workplace Violence Prevention

We experience the pain of workplace violence explosively, locally, immediately—but in truth it is a large-scale, wide-ranging problem that requires our collaboration and collective intelligence. How many times have we discovered that an active shooter had a history of mental illness or psychological disturbance, yet had no problems obtaining firearms, and no reporting of his or her condition to the authorities? Systemic failures, lack of communication, and large-scale systems not in place leave us unprotected. The consequence for the innocent and the bystander can be injury or death.

This situation is simply not acceptable as it stands. It is not something that can be remedied by a magic wand in Washington or by some state government or any one entity. It requires new thinking, collective action and collaboration. We need to build new tools and infrastructure, such as a national screening database for workplace violence, as well as develop new ideas to enhance worksite protection, create specialized workplace violence hotlines and to coordinate background information. I discuss these and other hard-policy directions in Chapter 10 of this book.

What I am really talking about is "breakthroughs" in creating new winning attitudes about workplace violence. The larger challenge for next practices in managing workplace violence is to break out of status-quo inertia and helplessness.

Following are some of the key elements that define what next practices for workplace violence will look like in action.

1. **Leadership:** Define a direction and align employees to build a culture that will deal with workplace violence.

2. **Engagement:** Communicate the message and engage all employees in the message, the goals and the culture.

3. **Individual Growth:** Encourage individual growth and commitment to the culture. This will help ensure that individuals are empowered to appropriately react to lower-level incidents while helping to prevent higher level-ones.

4. **Shared Responsibility:** Encourage a culture of shared responsibility in which everyone must collaborate and be involved in realizing the collective goals.

5. **Safety and Accountability:** Create a safe workplace for the individual. It is good for the organization and helps maintain integrity and brand value.

What really distinguishes next-practice thinking is that it is not just collaborative in the conventional sense, but that it combines the multi-disciplinary expertise of numerous parties and interests to create a solution that's greater than the sum of its parts.

ROUNDTABLE
Looking at Current Workplace Violence Prevention Practices

Bill Whitmore, *Chairman & CEO, AlliedBarton Security Services*
Chris Swecker, *former Assistant Director, Criminal Investigative Division, FBI*
Bonnie Michelman, *Director of Police and Outside Services, Massachusetts General Hospital*
Maureen Rush, *Vice President for Public Safety, University of Pennsylvania*
Patrick J. Wolfe, *former Vice President for Corporate Security, CIGNA Corporation, retired U.S. Secret Service*

Bill Whitmore: We want to explore how we can collaborate to get some better understanding of next practices for workplace violence prevention. Are there any gaps that you see in what is considered today's best practices, and where do you think they may be falling short?

Bonnie Michelman: I think that follow-up needs to be emphasized more. People may have good plans and good responses—they may even do good things after an incident, but whether that is really measured in terms of the implementation of solutions to improve quality and sustain effective preventative measures, I think that some of us may miss the boat.

Chris Swecker: We've talked about the "silent approach"—the reluctance of some organizations to proactively deal with the workplace violence threat because of fear of the message it might send. That is a gap because of a general reluctance to deal with it on the part of the first-line manager or even the next-line manager.

Patrick J. Wolfe: When I began educating the corporation on workplace violence in the early 1990s, it was considered very intrusive to do background checks and drug testing. It was a long process to get support from all the parties involved in these procedures, and the taskforce approach proved to be very effective. Now the team there responds quickly and effectively, and continues to drill with test situations and instituting updated communication policies.

Michelman: I think that every HR is different, and practices have progressed more in some places than in others, such as background screening, for example—it's the right thing to do for all new employees.

Whitmore: We know from our background screening business that certain states have passed laws that it is illegal to put certain questions on applications. For example, Philadelphia just passed a city ordinance that you cannot ask anyone at their first interview about their criminal background.

Michelman: You can't put it on an application in Massachusetts as of January.

Whitmore: You have all these laws that are passed without a true understanding of the issues.

Michelman: It's definitely creating land mines for us to be able to effectively prevent workplace violence.

Rush: This goes back to the timely warning that the federal government has required of universities. Don't investigate to see if it's true, just spread the word that there's a shooting. Don't worry about doing the tactical stuff, worry about the communications because you have people in the rooms tweeting each other. The argument now is how quickly you have to do it.

Wolfe: But get it right. When Osama Bin Laden was killed, the administration's first statement on exactly what happened was 90 percent wrong and then started getting refined and refined. We consider ourselves communicators, so before we make statements, recognizing that the pressure is considerable, let's get the facts.

Taking a Top-Down Approach to Workplace Violence Prevention

Companies sometimes try to marginalize workplace violence as an HR problem, as if the whole thing can be written off as an unfortunate hire. In reality, workplace violence is a companywide, systemic issue that can be strongly impacted, for better or worse, by the core culture of the organization itself, with HR as an important facilitator and support platform of policies and procedures to address it.

Dealing with workplace violence begins at the top, at the c-suite. The signals from the CEO and senior leadership on workplace violence are critical in how the company culture reacts.

A culture that tolerates minor incidents—sweeping them under the rug, making no attempt to learn from them and even less of an attempt to create a secure and safe environment for its employees—is creating an environment of risk for itself and for its own future.

Senior leadership can have a definitive impact on communicating the company culture, attitudes and expectations about workplace violence. This is where a culture of zero tolerance for bullying and verbal abusiveness and disrespect begins—from the top down. When employees know these lower-level forms of violence and disrespect are not to be tolerated, it changes the inner dynamic of the company. I feel very strongly that the more a company manages the milder forms of workplace violence, such as bullying, and intimidating behaviors, the more successfully that company will reduce or eliminate its exposure to higher-order abusive and violent behaviors.

Next Practices and Leadership

One cliché we all recognize for a really bad leader is the person who is surrounded by yes-men. So the first thing I look for in next practices for leadership is just the opposite: I look for leaders who are not afraid of engagement with challenging peers, and who can handle working with cross-functional teams.

The hallmark of next-practice thinking is to break out of silos and not get stuck in narrow, patterned, or lockstep ways of thinking. Here's an example: In the past, companies might have loaded all the responsibility to manage workplace violence incidents—including bullying, intimidation and abusive behaviors—onto managers and supervisors, and heavily discouraged reporting such incidents. From a next practices perspective, I want senior leaders to work with managers and supervisors to educate their employees to report such incidents. Why? Because only by building that level of culture of zero tolerance will you ultimately defeat workplace violence in your company, protecting your employees and the brand.

Next practices means changing the point of view and working together transparently. No closed doors and no shuttered windows. Keep things open, with everybody participating—executives, managers, employees— and all the lights on. Then real leadership can take place and we can all make our workplaces safer.

Next Practices and Employees

Most companies have an employee-engagement program. The only question is whether they give anything more than lip service to it or not. Everybody knows what he or she should do with employees; the question is whether they actually do it.

I know that one way to help prevent workplace violence is to get employees engaged. If you combine that concept with collaborative and cross-functional next practices thinking, there are many ways your employees can make meaningful contributions to creating a safe workplace for your company.

The fundamental next-practice for engaging your employees is real two-way communication. Just passing out the company handbook and policies isn't enough; you have to have clear open channels for dialog. As I described the leadership challenges above, part of the shift means empowering employees as part of a zero-tolerance culture on workplace violence as portrayed in the workplace violence continuum. To make that engagement real, you have to have a means to listen and hear what employees are saying when situations arise, even if it's inconvenient, even if tough and ugly situations have to be managed.

The continuum itself is a good example of a next-practices model, as it shows key behavior ranges that we can recognize, and it gives us the basis to assign responses to each of the behaviors by members of cross-functional teams.

What's important here is to be genuine with your employees. They have a right to a safe workplace, and you should genuinely engage them in creating it. A safe workplace is not just a pat on the head and some public relations.

Generating Creative Ideas

I think "creativity" is just another way of saying "keeping your edge" in the marketplace. Companies and individuals that stop generating creative ideas have become static, complacent, and irrelevant and in the final analysis, vulnerable.

Next-practice thinking is a way of moving forwrd and keeping the organization on its toes. Status-quo thinking is where you may be now—your boundaries. The goal is always to break out, enabling new ways to see your marketplace, your opportunities and new ways to address your challenges. As I noted earlier, the two main components of next-practice development are to do the following:

1. Deconstruct your situation through tasks such as risk analysis to see the moving parts of the challenges you have to face.

2. Build on that base of recognition to create models, frameworks and tools, like the workplace violence continuum, which helps you to see your challenges in new ways.

Different points of view can lead to alternative ways to resolve situations and forge creative solutions to problems. In my view, the best way to go about generating these ideas is to create several strong creative teams—not just one or two. Several overlapping cross-functional teams will give a voice to key people within and outside your company. The more points of view, the better. Creativity is not and should not be an orderly or a pretty process. It is always best when it is edgy and disruptive, with a lot of points of view on the table.

An essential piece of generating creative ideas is listening, gathering and facilitating. No matter how many great ideas you can put on the table, they have no value unless you can harvest them and distill out what's really valuable. I find that people from professional disciplines other than my own often have an entirely different mindset than I do when they're looking at a business situation or a problem related to workplace violence. Their priorities, assumptions and areas of focus are sometimes a long way from mine, and the types of solutions they emphasize can be dramatically different.

Creative ideas are important because they help us break out of our individual status-quo assumptions and into potential next practices by seeing a new way to enter a problem, a new approach to modeling a situation, or a new way to engage people to work on a situation collaboratively. To make creativity happen, you need to constantly challenge, listen to all ideas, read about and learn the work of others and reward creativity whenever and wherever it happens.

Establishing Internal Programs to Support Your Culture

To establish an exceptional workplace violence program, one that goes beyond the accepted or customary, your organization must create and nurture a culture designed to help managers and employees deal with the realities. Next-practices thinking and methods are key elements in building such a culture and reinforcing it in the day-by-day in the life of the company.

The starting point for this culture, and the programs that drive it is to defeat the isolation that correlates to workplace violence.

* In place of isolation, we must create community.

* In place of ignorance, we must disseminate knowledge.

* In place of insecurity and confusion, we must foster confidence.

The effort should begin with one or two anchor tools or points of reference. The workplace violence continuum is one of my favorite examples. It is a great illustration of a simple next practices framework tool. It provides a platform for understanding potential workplace violence events. It's not an absolute, hard definition, but provides everyone who sees it with a solid way to visualize, understand and differentiate these levels of intensity and put them into a larger and more effective picture.

With this tool in hand, you can build effective programs that take recognition and prevention to the next level. Working in groups, you can discuss the appropriate and safe responses when employees or groups of employees encounter a situation, or when one of these behaviors is displayed by another employee. What is the appropriate intervention or communication? What are the immediate personal safety considerations? How should risk be assessed and understood? These are difficult situations and you will have to assess them differently. Your programs will have to be flexible and open to interpretation.

Similarly, one of the greatest ways to strengthen your culture in dealing with workplace violence is through ongoing refreshment of learning, development, engagement and community around the workplace violence policies you have in place. The more you maintain these communications and use them to foster individual senses of belonging, the more you can convey confidence that you are taking a proactive stance on the safety of your employees.

Conveying that sense of safety through programs, next-practices initiatives, models and training is a fundamental element in your implementation of a culture against workplace violence. It contributes to the well-being of your employees, and to their sense of satisfaction in working for your company.

Hire for Fit

How do you hire the right people to execute these next practices and supporting programs? You need to always make sure that new hires will fit with the all-important culture you are creating. You need to "hire for fit." From my perspective, this means initially finding candidates who already have developed a reputation or track record for successful collaboration.

Dr. Mortimer Feinberg, a noted psychologist and author of the acclaimed book *Why Smart People Do Dumb Things*, is someone I have often turned to for guidance in building our strong, safe culture at AlliedBarton. He has listed 10 attributes that he sees as key for successful leaders, specifically those who can:

1. Be a pied piper, create a sense of mission.

2. Motivate others to join in the mission.

3. Create a sense of optimism—take your fears to the pillow.

4. Get measured results.

5. Demonstrate intellectual strength.

6. Create the capacity to tolerate ambiguity.

7. Develop a tolerance of risk.

8. Show the capacity for confrontation when necessary.

9. Possess an internal integrity compass.

10. Demonstrate curiosity and a willingness to grow intellectually.

Finding people who will embrace creativity and practice thinking, as well as productive culture building, requires methodical and attentive searches. These should include multiple "360"-degree interviews with all stakeholders, as well as meetings with employees, psychological assessments and more. With such people in place, workplace violence prevention can thrive.

Visualizing Future Situations

Organizations and their leaders are facing ever more complex challenges in an evolving marketplace, with technology evolution and other disruptive factors impacting the potential for workplace violence.

Next practice thinking can offer your organization the ability to better focus on modeling potential situations in your particular workplace, along with appropriate responses. Done right, you can anticipate future behaviors and align employees and managers as partners in dealing with workplace violence scenarios. Next-practices thinking augments your existing best practices, providing your organization and its people with effective tools to visualize future situations and develop best-in-class responses.

GUEST EXPERT
360-Degree Communication Is Crucial in Averting Workplace Violence

By J. Michael Coleman, *Vice President Marketing, Commercial Real Estate for AlliedBarton Security Services*

Workplace violence impacts everyone in the workplace—not just traditional, permanent employees, tenants and/or visitors. At AlliedBarton I focus on the commercial real estate sector, where forward-thinking property and facility managers are continually auditing their service providers and engaging in screening and background checks for their contracted vendors.

Fully engaged managers understand that tenant education programs and training help everyone understand the signs of potential workplace violence. This same paradigm can be applied to preventing workplace violence in any organizational setting.

Workplace violence prevention awareness is part of an overall communication process and should be an integral aspect of the orientation provided to those new to the property or workplace, with refresher classes provided on at least an annual basis to everyone. Concentrated training is advised for managers and first-line supervisors who are the eyes and ears of every organization. Physical drills bring the workplace violence plan to life and should include all service providers. A well-trained security team can help facilitate the drill.

Too often, managers and supervisors are unaware of workplace violence issues and are not prepared for the potential impact on the safety of the people who work under their purview. Understanding the behaviors that lead to workplace violence, and having the appropriate communication channels in place, is crucial to identifying possible workplace violence issues before they escalate into an event.

While issues such as evictions, harassment, non-payment and public nuisance are part and parcel of what my particular customers face, the broader perils of workplace violence have unfortunately become commonplace not only in commercial real estate, but also in most other industry sectors. This means that effective prevention plans should be commonplace as well. Your organization's leadership should be working in concert with an in-house or contract security provider to conduct a thorough threat analysis to determine the risk of workplace violence incidents at your place of business or on your property. Your team then can develop a plan of action to eliminate or mitigate the identified risks.

Regardless of industry sector, we all must constantly work to keep workplace violence a topic of priority with all parties involved. Adopting effective workplace violence avoidance policies demands that property managers, HR managers and senior executive teams alike keep current with pertinent municipal, county and state laws and practices, and develop relationships with local law enforcement. Equally important is to consider events or trends in the news and the local community in order to take full advantage of lessons learned in adopting the most meaningful approach to avoidance.

Leadership teams should continually educate themselves and those around them, review and update workplace violence prevention policies and ensure that policies are being actively practiced. Workplace violence prevention requires 360-degree communication and cooperation. Managers who work in concert with their colleagues, customers, service providers, security and law enforcement to proactively keep workplace violence at bay represent the finest leaders in their fields and the future standard of what will be expected from everyone.

Part Two

Enabling Your Secure Organization

chapter 5

Creating Security with Leadership

N umerous studies over the years have indicated a link between leadership and physical safety—,especially at job sites where there is a higher risk of accidents, such as at industrial facilities. What has been less examined is the relationship between solid leadership and workplace violence prevention.

The way I see it, strong and steady leadership is at the heart of workplace violence prevention. This is what I've always believed, and although we're not perfect, our own experience backs this up. I'll go even further: Any company that fails to embrace a leadership culture, with a definitive mandate on what defines leadership for each and every employee, will not achieve greatness, and will be more prone to an incident of workplace violence.

In this chapter I discuss how that connection between strong leadership values and safety works at AlliedBarton, and how it can be effective for you as well. I'll begin with our overall leadership philosophy and a high-level view of how we instill and nurture that culture. Then I'll address those connection points between strong leadership and workplace security. I'll wrap up with a rundown on our leadership programs—our "next practices"—and how they help to create a more secure workplace.

The Power of Leadership, Vision and Team

What separates the world's most admired and successful companies from those that are merely "doing well"? Well, the top executives at these businesses know from their own experience that leadership is essential. They understand that the best organizations are not "managed" to greatness; they are led there.

To be an effective leader, you can't just stand on a soapbox and preach. You need to assume *accountability* to your employees and your company, setting an example through your actions. If you do it right, your vision, values and leadership style will cascade down through the organization, making everyone more attuned to a cohesive, ethical culture that will fuel your success and keep you safe. Mentoring is a major element of this dynamic, as it breeds pride, ownership and a sense of being part of a team.

Last year I accompanied a group of friends on a flight to Boston to see the Flyers play the Bruins. It was a fundraiser, and I was happy to have so many people supporting the trip. We flew up together, had some Hall of Fame players on board and we all had a great time at the game.

AlliedBarton provides security services to the arena and as usual my antennae were up. I observed a very professional group of security officers and supervisors who were engaged with the fans. First of all, they were very well attired. Their uniforms were in great shape and they wore them with pride. The officers were helpful and friendly. Of course, I asked for directions and other information and every one of the officers was terrific. Best of all, they provided a great sense of security and safety while serving as outstanding customer service representatives.

They were very attuned to their jobs. When I asked them questions it was clear that they really knew what they were doing, and you could tell that there was a real *esprit de corps* at their workplace—they obviously shared the same vision and sense of purpose. Their interactions with each other were also top notch—they were truly engaged with one another. Great leaders create an emotional connection with people, and you could see that at their workplace.

At some point, I started to introduce myself and as you can imagine, word got out that I was visiting the arena for the game. I quickly realized that they were great leaders. At the time, I didn't really know these employees, but I made of point of talking to them through the evening. Now here's what's really interesting: As I was speaking with them they told me what a great leaders *their* direct supervisors are. This simply serves to illustrate that superb leaders create more great leaders. Great leadership is contagious. What's more, great leaders make any work environment come alive as they instill core values through examples that filter throughout the organization. That's what this is all about.

During the game, I eventually met their senior managers, Jim Mayall, the account manager, and Bill Corcoran, the event manager, and it was very obvious why we have such a great team at the arena. Jim and Bill are professional all the way. I could clearly see why our folks thought so highly of them and why our employees are so engaged in the protection and safety of the fans. Jim and Bill were one hundred percent engaged as well. It is contagious!

I was at a social event a couple of weeks later with many of the same people who went on the trip to the hockey game. They were raving about the AlliedBarton employees who they encountered at the arena and what great people they were. "You should have seen the people who work for Bill's company," they said, clearly impressed. Of course, I was very impressed as well.

Obviously, the point here is that workplace violence prevention through leadership starts at the top; it involves everyone. Leadership qualities can be embodied by any employee at any level. This is particularly important in an organization such as ours, where many account-level employees are directly charged with securing the people, property and assets of our customers.

To assure that we address our primary business mission to the highest possible standard, we provide continual training and learning opportunities, this ensures that leadership values are embraced at all levels of our company. Training and leadership are key to executing often complex missions at diverse job sites, so we look to our security professionals as leaders, as they are an important part of a facility's or community's safety and security—working in conjunction with local law-enforcement personnel, fire fighters and emergency medical responders.

Workplace violence prevention starts at the top, taking a people-first approach to leadership, but it involves everyone, because any employee can grow to become a valued leader.

Engaged Leadership, Safety and Success

There's a direct connection between engaged leadership, workplace security and organizational success, regardless of your product or service. Psychologist Abraham Maslow identified safety and security as among the most basic human needs on the road to self-actualization—achieving one's full potential. It therefore follows that if your employees don't feel safe and secure, they're not going to do the best job for you. Even the lower levels of workplace violence can create that insecurity, so good leadership is critical to creating a safe, high-achieving workplace.

Our own experience shows that where there is a culture of leadership engagement—where leaders are seen as plugged in and responsive to their employees;

where employees feel that their leaders are concerned with their everyday activities, personal well-being and overall security—those are the places where you see engaged employees on every level along with higher morale.

A nationwide scientific survey that AlliedBarton conducted in May 2011 revealed that workers who either experienced or are aware of violence or the conditions leading to it at their workplace rate their current place of employment *lower* in most respects than those in violence-free workplaces. Among the details:

- ✦ When comparing employees who have experienced or are aware of workplace violence with those who have not shared this experience, there are substantial differences. Fifty-eight percent of those who are aware of violence in their workplace strongly agree they feel valued. By contrast, 70 percent of those who haven't experienced violence in their workplace have the same attitude.

- ✦ Workplace violence also affects an employee's view of compensation. Our survey found that 55 percent of those who have not experienced or are not aware of workplace violence strongly agree they are paid fairly. However, only about one in three (36 percent) of those who are aware of some form of violence at work share this attitude. Does this imply that their pay isn't worth the risk they perceive, or is it a reflection of their overall feeling of value? Our survey didn't drill down to that level, but either way it doesn't reflect good employee morale and engagement.

Clearly, workplace violence can impact morale, turnover and bottom line. But what is the leadership connection? It's right here:

- ✦ Our survey also shows that employees *who have not reported violence or a related event* are more likely to say their employer makes safety a top priority. In essence, the reasonable conclusion to be drawn is that when employers show concern with workplace violence, the actual number of incidents is likely to decline. When workplace violence declines, greater benefits follow.

The following chart shows the difference in workplace violence incidents when leadership is engaged, and when they're not.

Leadership can always be more proactive, and that increases the chances of heading off workplace violence. Recently we had an employee displaying

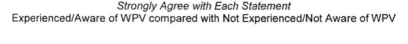

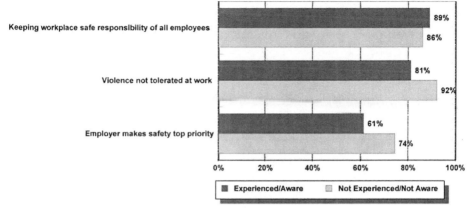

AlliedBarton's survey uncovered some interesting attitudes toward workplace violence.

all of the characteristics of an individual who felt that life had beaten him down and that there was no hope. Although he did not threaten personal harm to others, he was projecting all of the typical indicators we associate with a possible threat for workplace violence: he was despondent, felt alone, left out and that his world was coming to an end. He had relationship and financial problems as well.

I was advised of the situation by Ron Rabena, President of AlliedBarton's East Division. Ron's approach was to do everything we could to help this individual while keeping the company safe. We brought in employee assistance to assist him. Our HR folks got involved to help him as well. No one will ever know if this situation could have escalated, but employees on the job took the time and expended the effort to show leadership. They stepped up and got involved.

Bear in mind that it was people at the account level—those who focus specifically on protecting our clients—who originally brought this to our attention. These frontline individuals, because of their training and because of the engaged leadership they exhibited, identified this person and took the critical initiative. I was really proud of our employees in that instance. Instead of just saying "Hey, we've got a problem here; we've got to remove this guy," they said "we've got to help this person."

Motivation

The rub for most organizations and their leadership teams is that it's easy to be complacent in the absence of a workplace violence incident. The typical attitude of "it can't happen here" is pervasive. In these cases, protecting against workplace violence is a question of motivation, or a lack thereof, on the part of an organization's leaders and those who report to them.

Of course measuring the lack of incidents at any given workplace is an exercise in comparison. You have to consider the norm for an industry in terms of incidents, and then compare that to the records of organizations with various leadership cultures and employee perceptions about leadership.

One of the interesting discussions from an external leadership circle held this year at our headquarters was that you never see numbers associated with the success of preventative measures. As an example, a disgruntled employee who was considering committing an act of workplace violence may have been dissuaded due to the preventative measures being deployed. That one prevented incident will never appear on a statistical analysis. So when people think that "It can't happen here," is that because of the protective culture in place, or that tactics have worked? In some instances it could be just luck of the draw, but I believe that these measures do work.

Creating and sustaining such motivation requires special leadership skills, which may differ from those required to fulfill other business-focused goals. Still, there is great commonality in purpose, because workplace violence prevention is essential to ensuring the protection of shareholders investments and company assets. It comes down to ownership of the full spectrum of risks that exist, and accountability to your company's employees and shareholders.

Two-Way Communication

Communications is at the center of everything we do at AlliedBarton. It's always important to make the time to communicate your vision and culture through face-to-face meetings with your managers and employees. High levels of reliable communication between leadership and an organization's workforce supports trust, engagement and motivation—all factors essential to effective workplace violence prevention.

One of our petrochemical customers is well known for its major focus on safety and security. At this particular company, working safely is a core value—a philosophy that is shared by the leadership team and consistently communicated to its employees and contractors. They routinely collect detailed information about safety incidents while constantly analyzing "near misses" to improve their knowledge and understanding of workplace safety dynamics. Then they convey what they know, again and again, to every employee. It works for them, and will work for every organization.

Good communication like this should be frequent, straightforward and positive, coupled with respect for employees professionalism and with demonstrations of concern for them personally. Employees at organizations where these attributes are an integrated part of the culture tend to feel that they are appreciated as individuals and that their contributions are valued.

I believe that it's very important to get to know our managers personally so that I can properly direct them when they come to me with a question or a concern. Someone posed a question to me one time about safety concerns at the site of a particular client—a place where our employees might be exposed to personal risk. Employees and managers alike spoke to me about this, and inevitably they said, "I'm really debating this. It's a big client, a lot of money, but in my gut, I'm a little worried."

After listening to their concerns, I directed them to the value statement that is distributed to all of our employees, *Dare to be GREAT*, which in fact states our principle that the customers and the workplaces we choose should match our core values, not the other way around. We should never compromise our values, including those related to workplace safety, in order to bend to what might otherwise be an attractive business opportunity. I told this person that the answer is in the booklet, and we ended up not taking that piece of business. I further discuss *Dare to be GREAT* later in this chapter.

Many of our company's senior leaders and managers began their careers with AlliedBarton. Those who have worked their way up to management or executive positions do not hesitate to proactively communicate—reaching out and helping others do the same.

That's important because it's very tough to get everyone to look from the same lens in an organization. The solution for this is to continue to communicate. For years I've been holding breakfast focus groups with key leaders in our various field offices—talking to them about the company, what it means to be here, and expectations. I try to keep each discussion fairly intimate, with no more than 10 people. I introduce myself, talk about the company, our mission, and get their feedback and questions. This fosters a sense of trust and being part of a team among my regional leaders, assuring that we're all on the same page and comfortable sharing important perspectives with one another. It helps me become a better leader as well.

We have an open-door policy for any issues that may bubble up or any problems that people are having. A disgruntled employee could lead to a problem, so all of AlliedBarton's leaders' email addresses are available to our staff on our internal website. If there's something anyone wants to discuss, he or she can email his or her direct manager, or even me, and we will get on top of the issue. This opens up communication even further and gives people throughout the organization a voice.

The Trust Factor

Interpersonal trust between leaders and their employees is another key factor in creating a safe, secure workplace, especially as organizations have become flatter and more team-based. Acclaimed organizational theorist and author Chris Argyris and many others have shown that trust is a significant influencing factor with variables such as the quality of communication, individual performance and growth, problem solving and overall cooperation.

Leadership's effectiveness depends more than ever on the ability to gain the trust of the people who work for them. It also assumes that the one holding the trust, the employee, will perform certain desired behaviors, and that the leader has both the desire and the ability to "walk the talk."

So trust works both ways: Employees considered to be trustworthy behave in ways expected of them with little or no supervision, and are more supportive of and committed to both their leaders and the overall organization. They also are likely to be more satisfied with their position in the organization, more loyal and committed to its goals, and more willing to behave in ways that help to further those ideals—all essential factors in mitigating the risk of workplace violence.

In the 1995 research publication "An Integrated Model of Organizational Trust," researchers Roger Mayer, James H. Davis and F. David Schoorman found that three leadership factors—ability, benevolence and integrity—mapped to employees' perceptions of trustworthiness. Ellen M. Whitener went down much of the same research path and in 1998 published her view that those trust factors could be categorized as behavioral consistency, behavioral integrity, sharing and delegation of control, open and accurate communication, and demonstration of concern.

Organizational Support

Another key link between leadership and workplace violence prevention is organizational support—ensuring that your organization's values reflect and support the actions and behaviors you're requesting from your workers. Perhaps the most important factor in nurturing this dynamic is leadership's show of commitment and involvement, as employees' perceptions of organizational support has been shown in several studies, including our own survey, to be significantly related to their willingness to engage in security-related communication with superiors.

Walking the Talk

At AlliedBarton, leadership is much more than a corporate slogan or philosophy. We see it as essential to daily service delivery at all locations and with every interaction with customers and the general public.

Here especially, we feel that we must demonstrate initiative—leading our mission to protect people, property and assets. Whether in the case of a frontline security officer assisting with a lost child or a manager developing emergency procedures for a new client site, the urgency for leadership is the same. It's the same for your company as well, regardless of your particular industry, impacting not only how well you perform, but how safe your company will be. I could point to many product and service companies that have built world-renowned leadership brands.

One is Hilton Hotels under CEO Chris Nassetta, who this past year was honored as "International Hotelier of the Year." Hilton apparently has really been working hard with its team in building strong leadership, and the company's efforts pay off day after day. It shows. As a frequent traveler, I can always be assured of being served by friendly, courteous and helpful Hilton employees.

The U.S. Coast Guard is a different type of organization that, in my view, has elevated its leadership culture to notable heights. The men and women of the Coast Guard take their job seriously. They are proud of their organization, its history and mission, and carry out their responsibilities professionally. These folks help to educate boaters about safety and environmental issues, rescue mariners and fishermen and play a vital role in our national security. Although I have no personal knowledge about the details of their leadership and development programs within the Coast Guard, I have been very impressed with the qualities they have exhibited whenever I have had personal interactions with them.

If you look closely at either of these, you'll see that, in each case, their organizational culture is one of growth and engagement, and one where their leadership culture lights the way for next practices that encourage workforce alertness, cohesion and safety.

Next Practices for Building Great Leadership

Of course, I'm not perfect and therefore I try to improve myself all the time. Like anything for which you want to become an expert, great leadership takes focus and practice. Great leadership that serves the cause of workplace violence prevention with motivation, communication, trust and organizational support is even a bit more nuanced. Even so, the effort is worth it. Developing and nurturing these attributes with actionable programs that engage every employee can turn out to be the best thing you ever have done for your organization. Let me tell you a bit about how we address these priorities here at our company.

Developing Leaders

Our ongoing commitment to our leadership culture and to developing leaders throughout the organization is woven throughout everything we do. We believe in providing continual training and learning opportunities that ensure that our employees embrace opportunities for leadership.

A major part of leadership is building and communicating your culture to your employees, and when it comes to that, I believe that you should do it early and shouldn't leave anything to chance. You need to make very clear what you expect from your colleagues, and make sure that they understand that the company will support them as they do their jobs and take a proactive approach to preventing workplace violence.

Dare to be GREAT

Employee development is the hallmark of the AlliedBarton culture. Leadership development begins as early as recruiting as we look to align individuals who we believe can successfully lead our mission. From there, the journey is launched immediately. Each new employee at AlliedBarton receives a copy of our employee value statement, the *Dare to be GREAT Blueprint for Success*. It outlines our core values and philosophy pertaining to leadership, vision and teamwork, and achieving greatness. It emphasizes our outlook of being results-oriented, customer-centered, focused, disciplined, proactive and agile with a "can do" mentality.

In fact, these values are incorporated in the acronym used in the title:

GROWTH: Encouraging individual, team and organizational growth.

RESPONSIBILITY: Honoring our service commitment to customers, employees and the community.

EMPOWERMENT: Offering development programs that enable employees to do their jobs with skill and confidence.

ACHIEVEMENT: Rewarding and recognizing service excellence, team success and individual achievement.

TRUST: Building trust, respect and integrity in every relationship and interaction.

This same document also highlights the core purpose of our organization, which is to serve and secure the people, homes and businesses of our communities. In it we detail our ideal culture and provide management, operational and security officer mandates that we all strive to live by.

For our leadership in particular, we ask for the following:

+ Lead by example.

+ Promote and embody our culture, values and beliefs with passion.

+ Assume ownership for our company's success.

+ Develop your employees.

+ Take ownership of issues and proactively find solutions.

+ Take responsibility and do the right thing.

+ Project energy and enthusiasm.

+ Remember that you are part of a team and have a responsibility to everyone on it.

Our leaders live and work by those principles, and making leadership part of our company's formal employee development process helps to keep the focus on this important topic ongoing at all levels, connecting leadership to all aspects of employees' responsibilities.

I always call *Dare to be GREAT* a challenge, because nobody is perfect, and nobody is going to be perfect at this. However, the employee response to this challenge has been phenomenal: Over 40,000 individual employees have gone on our website to pledge themselves to our *Dare to be GREAT* principles. I think they understand that simply striving to conduct yourself according to these principles, you're going to grow and get better at what you do—not only as a leader and an effective employee of our company, but as a human being.

Leadership Boot Camps

Our leaders are responsible for career development, performance and care. Periodically we hold leadership "boot camps" where we create a memorable experience for all levels of management, getting them together, talking, sharing stories and working on leadership issues. Our primary goal is to engage them around all aspects of leadership. As with most organizations, everyone focuses on the day-to-day requirements of serving customers, and it is easy to forget the responsibilities that we accept as leaders. Let's face it—we all have lots of measurements on productivity, profitability and cost controls. Key performance indicators for leadership are frequently regarded as a once-a-year HR program. So we like to revitalize the entire leadership team, reminding them that great leaders foster engaged employees. Engaged employees are more content in the workplace and serve customers better.

Leadership boot camps and other programs focused on building an engaged leadership team are the most important issues facing any corporate leader. At these meetings personal interaction is a top priority. We want these issues to be focused on the concerns of our people. To maximize the return on the invested time and effort, we'll send out a survey to attendees in advance to find out what's on their mind and to help us build an agenda around key issues.

I'll open each boot camp with a town hall meeting where I'll brief those attending on the state of the company, answer any questions they may have about what we're doing and where we're going, and what we're going to focus on. We may look at a customer survey, analyze the results and talk about what we can do to get even better scores. Typically we'll have a notable guest speaker and an award and recognition program.

We mix up the agenda fairly well to challenge and involve everyone. At every step, we're trying to foster a sense of teamwork and let people know they're empowered to act on behalf of the company. As a nationwide company with over one hundred offices, fostering teamwork and communication is always a part of the agenda and a major challenge.

Over the years, my wife and I have hosted many dinners at our home with managers. These dinners make the entire event more intimate and foster a caring, family feeling. Storytelling is a terrific leadership tool and these types of events present the perfect opportunity to share the best.

Management Thoughts from our *Dare to be GREAT Blueprint for Success*

* Recognize someone doing something right.
* The conventional definition of management is getting things done through people, but real management is developing people through work.
* One of the best indicators of a culture of accountability is when employees routinely "own" their decisions, their missteps and their shortcomings.
* The fastest, smartest way to achieve accountability is to manage people, not numbers.
* The most effective managers know when to lead and when to manage.
* Engaged employees assume ownership.
* Good management consists of motivating ordinary employees to accomplish extraordinary results.
* An employee's supervisor has more impact on that employee's growth, productivity and energy than any other manager regardless of their position or title.
* The primary responsibility of a manager is to lead, motivate and develop his or her team.

Mentoring

I'm really proud of how many people in this company have developed into leaders, and to a large degree that has come from mentoring. Those who have worked their way up to management or executive positions should always be encouraged to reach out and help others do the same. Mentoring is invaluable, as you can see from the story of the trip to Boston. When someone sets a leadership example, engaged employees tend to follow, and there's nothing better than growing through observation and consultation with someone who has shown the skills to lead.

Here informal mentoring takes place from the very start of an employee's career. Introduced in 2008, a program of ours called SAIL (Security Academy in Leadership) includes formal meetings, training sessions and day-to-day interactions between mentors and protégés. Mentors/protégés are nominated by their leadership team. Results have been great.

Other mentoring programs continue to be deployed. At a recent leadership program we implemented a Peer Mentoring Network designed to provide career development tools. The objective of the network is to foster an inclusive, mentoring culture where colleagues are encouraged to select their advisers based on respect and recognition of expertise. The program was structured by encouraging participants to build a profile that included areas of strengths and development opportunities. Participants matched themselves based on need. Sample agenda items include work/life balance, managing upward and overcoming obstacles.

And then there is more personalized mentoring. During my career in law enforcement and security, I've been fortunate to have had several great managers who offered me leadership and mentorship. While I'm CEO today, I treasure my mentor relationships with past supervisors, and we even hired Frank Rodrique, who served as my Sergeant at the Upper Merion Township, Pennsylvania Police Department more than three decades ago, to work as a quality assurance manager at AlliedBarton because of his caring attitude, mentoring and trust—he cares.

Another exemplary AlliedBarton leader is James S. Wood, who serves as our account manager for a community college in Maryland. A United States Army Sergeant, police officer and member of the National Guard, Wood returned from military tours in Iraq and Afghanistan to provide leadership to a loyal cadre of more than 30 supervisors and officers. Wood leads his team by example with a focus on training, discipline and a commitment to outstanding customer service.

"Through training and day-to-day management, our team embraces its leadership roles in a culture that is dedicated to providing outstanding customer service," Wood says. "My team knows I will not ask them to do anything that I am not willing to do myself. Dragging your feet is not what a client wants. If you have a problem, you address it, tell the client how it will be resolved and work toward solving the problem."

Training and quality leadership also are reflected in the heroic actions of our officers on the job. Security Officer James Cariddi, for example, responded quickly when a vehicle carrying two infants went into the Connetquot River that flows along the Dowling College campus in New York State. The two infants were rescued by Cariddi, a retired corrections officer from the New York City Department of Corrections. He cares.

It's no accident that our people are the best in the industry. Whether it is a natural disaster that requires the actions of many and a coordinated team effort, or a single security officer on patrol at a mall who goes out of his way to help a customer burdened with packages, the result of a leadership culture is evident in the performance and attitude of our officers.

A Leadership Path for Everyone

Leadership opportunities abound for people who use the tools and resources at their disposal. Just ask Mimi Lanfranchi, who joined Allied-Barton 10 years ago as a Vice President of Business Development, has served as Vice President/General Manager and now is Senior Vice President of National Accounts. According to Mimi, "An organization of our size, that is geographically dispersed with employees at client sites, branch offices, satellite sites and virtual offices, demands that employees clearly understand what is expected of them and make the most of all the training opportunities that are offered." She's absolutely correct.

ROUNDTABLE
Leadership and Workplace Violence

Bill Whitmore, Chairman & CEO, *AlliedBarton*
Rich Cordivari, *Vice President National Accounts, AlliedBarton*
Chris Swecker, *Security Consultant, and former Assistant Director Criminal Investigative Division, FBI*
Patrick J Wolfe, *former Vice President for Corporate Security, CIGNA Corporation, retired U.S. Secret Service*

Bill Whitmore: Engaged leaders don't produce an environment where there is bullying and intimidation, or where there are any incidents of violence. They just don't tolerate it. At the same time, we need to get organizational leaders to start thinking about projecting a caring attitude. If you see an employee who is really having issues, make sure it's apparent that you care to help them out. Either way, how do you think we make sure that leadership is more engaged?

Rich Cordivari: One way is making sure that management and c-suite leaders in the company are living the engagement value and not just saying it, and then making sure that that a caring attitude is reinforced in the employee base from day one. This says to employees "I care about you and your safety is important."

Patrick J. Wolfe: I think that is a function of creating comfort in an organization so that when you see something and then say something, somebody is going to act on it. I think it's human nature to say "The heck with it, I'm not going to tell anybody because they are not going to do anything." You've got to battle that, and that's a leadership issue.

Bill Whitmore: Security experts should partner with HR in our effort to prevent workplace violence by fostering these leadership values. That takes a while and I think success ultimately depends on the executive — whether or not they are engaged or aware of what's going on. So a large part of it is the culture — the exposure from management.

Chris Swecker: Many don't want workplace violence associated with their brand, so they may be inclined to minimize the visibility of their prevention program. Also, executives often tend to think it's a law enforcement issue. They are so far downstream from where the rubber meets the road... and where *does* the rubber meet the road at the supervisory level inside the organization? Where do you get the most good for your corporate effort? You have only so much time and attention that they are willing to devote to this, so where do you spend it? That seems to be the focus.

Leadership–Employee Factors in Forging Workplace Security

It's one thing to talk in high-level terms about the value of leadership in workplace violence prevention. It's another to make a practice of leadership skills that will pay dividends day after day. The following table may serve as a useful reference to evaluate your company's own interpersonal interactions in the workplace.

EMPLOYEE LEVEL	THEMES	SPECIFIC ATTITUDES AND ACTIONS
SENIOR LEADERSHIP	Attitudes toward workplace violence prevention	✦ Views engaged, educated and enabled employees as key to both safety and business success
	Leadership style	✦ Full communication with employees ✦ Open-door policy ✦ "Walks the talk"
	Vision	✦ Clearly articulate responsibility and potential for every person to proactively support workplace violence prevention standards
	Engagement	✦ Connect with employees, showing respect and concern for their views and well-being
	Trust	✦ Committed to building trust with employees, with demonstrable results
MIDDLE MANAGEMENT	Commitment to workplace violence prevention	✦ Resources given to security policy and enforcement
	Leadership style	✦ Full communication with employees ✦ Open-door policy ✦ "Walks the talk"
	Relationships	✦ Personal knowledge of employees concerns ✦ Demonstrates concern for employee' well-being
	Communication	✦ Open-door policy ✦ Encourages communication and honest exchange of views ✦ Encourages feedback and suggestions
	Support	✦ Leading by example ✦ Open to suggestions ✦ Visibly supports enablement of employees
DIRECT SUPERVISOR	Enablement	✦ Open-door policy ✦ Encourages feedback ✦ Demonstrates fairness ✦ Recognizes achievement or sacrifice
	Involvement	✦ Walks the talk ✦ Participatory style ✦ Valuing the group
EMPLOYEE	Engagement	✦ Enabled to freely and consistently offer opinions ✦ Comfortable communicating with supervisor ✦ Actively engaged with organizational goals
	Attitude and understanding	✦ Recognition that prevention is everyone's job ✦ Awareness of warning signs ✦ Invested in company ✦ Sense of individual responsibility
	Enablement	✦ Feels motivated ✦ Understands goals and importance of program ✦ Understands warning signs ✦ Understands practices and tools available ✦ Buy-in to "see something, say something"

When Violence Happens

The idea that management should somehow be shielded from any kind of involvement after a workplace violence incident is a fallacy and a mistake. As a leader, how you act in the wake of workplace violence will speak volumes to the company—your employees, customers and stakeholders.

There seems to be a sort of hands-off attitude that I've observed, and I don't know why that is. For example, some time ago one of our security officers based in Florida was killed in the line of duty as he tried to prevent an unauthorized, unwanted individual from entering a residential gated community. For a number of reasons, I was unable to make it to the funeral, which not only bothered me personally, but also ran counter to my strongly held philosophy about leadership engagement. I was determined to do whatever was necessary to live up to my leadership ideals, which I felt were important.

So, a short time later I traveled to the city where the employee had lived, and we conducted a recognition program with his family. I was accompanied by our division president, Ron Rabena, and also brought the leadership of our office there. We reserved a private room in a restaurant, invited the officer's family and spoke with them. Everybody shared stories about what a wonderful individual our officer was, and that he was a hero. We presented the family with a plaque and named an award in his honor.

We did this because our employee deserved the recognition, though it also helped all of us — leadership and our employees — deal better with the tragedy. It strengthened our bonds with one another, and helped further our commitment to safety and engagement. It demonstrated that our leadership cared and that we were all pulling in the same direction to make our company safer and more successful.

Acting Boldly

Of course there always are legal considerations whenever an incident occurs. Still, there undoubtedly are times when leaders must be bold and step out from behind the layers of protection that may have been erected under the banner of "conventional wisdom." As with the recognition program for our fallen colleague, this is all about protecting the spirit of an organization. That, perhaps more than anything else, is incumbent upon its leadership.

People are so worried when something happens that they tend to think of the legal and risk-management considerations first, and they forget the fact that for the company the emotional toll is very high. Leadership may think "I'd better not comment" or "I'd better stay away from that." Leadership should not be removed, or take a strict legal/risk management approach to post-violence follow-up. All of the experts may be saying "You can't do this or that." However, you've got to step up and say "Look, my addressing the issue head-on and my speaking out frankly to our employees is not a negative. In fact, it's the right thing to do." Getting actively involved in the wake of workplace violence sends a powerful message to employees that you care and are involved, which strengthens the bonds of your organization going forward.

The Story in the Numbers

Our nationwide survey found that almost all (94 percent) of employers take some action as a result of workplace violence, but that the action taken usually was limited to meeting with employees. Seventy three percent of employees who witnessed, heard about or experienced workplace violence report their employer held an employee meeting and 69 percent say the employer met with the employee who experienced workplace violence.

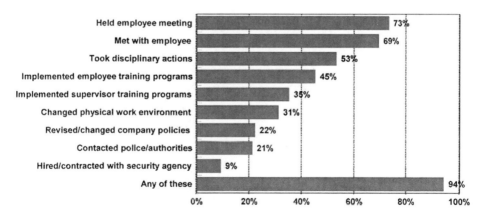

Actions taken by an employer as a result of workplace violence.

However, employers appear much less likely to take other actions when these events occur. Only about half (53 percent) took disciplinary actions. Even fewer implemented training programs for employees (45 percent) or for supervisors (35 percent). Changes to physical environments (31 percent) or revisions to company policies (22 percent) were even less common. Increasing security through the involvement of police or other authorities, or contracting with a security agency, were the actions least likely to be taken as a result of workplace violence.

This lack of specific actions taken as a result of workplace violence is reflected in the low level of involvement by senior managers when these events occur. Fewer than half (44 percent) of senior managers (CEO/president/owner) are perceived as being concerned with workplace violence, while only 17 percent were seen by our survey respondents as being "very concerned" about the issue.

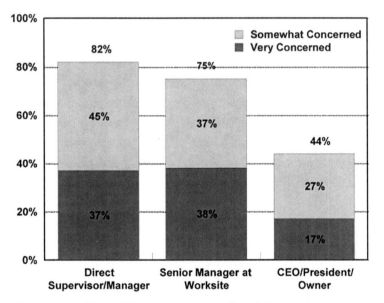

Those who witnessed, heard about or experienced workplace violence are very or somewhat concerned.

The Bottom Line

While the safety and well being of employees is of primary importance, there's also a direct financial argument for dealing personally and proactively with a workplace violence incident. A violent event can shake the confidence invested in your organization by employees, customers, close partners and of course shareholders. Even less violent levels of workplace violence, such as bullying and sexual harassment, can cause low productivity, high turnover and expensive litigation—all of which routinely cost organizations millions of dollars each year.

Leadership's immediate reaction to an event can be a key mitigating factor. Your ability to deal with the aftermath of an incident will reflect strongly on your skill in dealing with difficult circumstances generally, which will not only bolster morale, engagement and productivity, but will play heavily in your organization's ability to recover shareholder value and the confidence of all of your stakeholders.

Bottom line: You've got to act boldly and quickly, not only keeping a steady hand on the wheel, but showing commitment and passion for your employee base. Employees want to know that you care. By those experiences, you and the company will grow.

Look in the Mirror

As the company leader, chances are you are always asking yourself how your company can be more efficient, how your employees can do their jobs better, and how you can always do more to create that safe and secure environment. I know that I do that, and part of it involves looking in the mirror.

One of the traits I most admire in a president or CEO is curiosity. Good leaders are curious about themselves as much as — or even more so — than they are about the companies they run. If you're not curious about yourself, about others, about how to improve, about how things work, you may not have the right attitude for progressing.

As a good leader, you want frequent feedback on how you can perform better. Many years ago I attended a Covey leadership conference. Prior to the conference, I was given some 360-degree personal evaluation forms. I then sent them to everyone I know — family, friends, peers and employees, and asked that they return them anonymously. Yes, I detected some surprise when handing out the forms, but I explained myself. I told all of these people that I felt I knew how I performed and had my own ideas about how people perceived me. I added that I thought there would be some real value in discovering if I was really the person and leader I thought I was. After all, if you aren't a good leader in the eyes of those who follow you, then you aren't a good leader, period.

The idea, however, was not simply to find out whether I was "good" or "not so good" at what I do. What drove me in this instance was the belief that leadership has to start with self-awareness. All of the results were presented in chart form and the ideal was to have most of the results aligned with my own assessment. In my case, almost everyone's "dot" on the final evaluation analysis was right on top of mine, which was good news.

The people who manage this survey will tell you that there is always one person who is important to you who will see you in a significantly different light than you see yourself. Well, there was one individual whose analysis result was way off from mine. Although the survey was totally anonymous, I could tell by this one person's answers who he was. So, I went and spoke to him, and he was very upset that I had figured out his identity. I told him that it was obvious from his answers that they were his, and that I wasn't angry at all, but that I just wanted to understand why he saw me in a way that was so different from my self-assessment. It gave me the opportunity to have a conversation and build a better relationship.

Making Leadership a Priority

What if a CEO of a company set a tone and said "We do not condone any threats of workplace violence, bullying or intimidation. We highly encourage you to report it if you see it happening. The attitude around here is going to be that we have no tolerance for the threat of workplace violence or workplace intimidation. There's no place for it."

If you do that, your HR people may say "You can't bring that kind of stuff up," but leadership's got to make the point that this goes beyond optimizing your legal risk. It's not a perk, it's not a feel-good thing, it's not a risk-management issue. It's essential, and as a company you're not going to get to where you need to be until that is addressed. Then, if you create and encourage the organizational culture and support to ensure that this attitude grows in a responsible, engaged and productive way, you're well on your way to being both successful and secure.

GUEST EXPERT
Leadership as a Tool for Workplace Security

By David I. Buckman, Executive Vice President and General Counsel, AlliedBarton

Workplace violence is often the result of an employee feeling disengaged or harboring feelings of being poorly treated at work. Those feelings can readily emerge in a culture that lacks leadership and the capacity at all levels to provide appropriate engagement and guidance. Key to addressing this is an overall culture of strong leadership and communication.

When employees feel marginalized and disaffected, it's frequently a result of uncertainty and a sense of not having control. That can be exacerbated when leadership fails to provide employees the insight they need into how the company is doing and how the employee is performing, as well as the future outlook for the organization and their own positions. When there isn't clear and candid communication about these topics, employees' imaginations may start to take over, filling in the gaps in possibly detrimental ways. For someone with a certain mindset, these feelings can fester.

High-level leadership needs to provide regular, candid communication on all levels about how the company is doing—good or bad. In addition, the organization has to insist upon not only adherence to regular and formalized review processes, but also more informal one-on-one time between every manager and his or her employees. This gives managers an opportunity to check in with individual team members on a personal level, assess their feelings about their place at the company, and look for issues that might be going on in their life that could lead to a concern. Part of the inherent value in this is that when employees understand that there is an opportunity for effective two-way communication to air their concerns, they feel they have more control over their circumstances.

Leadership needs to encourage every employee to speak up if he or she has concerns about an individual or actually witnesses workplace violence. This requires an environment and processes that enable people to speak up. Just saying "See something, say something" is not enough. People need to know who to talk to and how the information is treated. They have to be enabled and made to feel comfortable through organizational support. Otherwise, they're going to hesitate, because reporting on a coworker requires that they step out of the cultural norm. The messaging, processes and understanding has to be powerful enough to overcome those cultural biases.

Leadership additionally must demonstrate a clear personal investment in workplace violence prevention and, when necessary, recovery. When communications around workplace violence prevention and response come from an organization's top leaders, they tend to resonate most strongly. The more personally vested the highest level appears to be in this issue, the better. It's one thing for someone's boss to say "We received this memo, and you have to go to the training." It's quite another when the CEO says "I've just completed the workplace violence training." The higher the level of the messenger, and the greater the perceived personal commitment, the more that message will be internalized by the employee.

That personal investment on the part of leadership is also important in the wake of an incident, when people need to know that the organization cares. Senior leadership needs to be onsite and communicating clearly and appropriately with employees, face to face. They need to be hands on in the recovery, post-incident counseling and support.

Overall, an organization that focuses on top-to-bottom leadership and on support for open communication will tend to minimize, mitigate and ultimately prevent the kind of festering issues that can result in workplace violence, and that's invaluable.

chapter 6

Nurture Employee Engagement

Workplace violence is committed by people, of course, and it also can be prevented by people, but in the latter case I'm not just talking about professional security personnel. In fact, the first line of defense in preventing most forms of workplace violence can be found in all of the individuals in your organization—and, most effectively, people who are engaged, educated and empowered by HR and all levels of management.

By "engaged," I mean in tune and committed to your organization's goals as well as to fellow employees. When I say "educated" I refer to those who have a track record of personal growth and improvement, regardless of any formal certificates or degrees they may have held when they entered the organization. And from my perspective, "empowered" means employees who are trained, encouraged and supported by the organization to report unusual or threatening behavior by their colleagues. This outlook goes to the heart of organizational culture. You could call this the "3E" approach, and it's my overriding focus in the next few chapters.

Steven M. Crimando, Managing Director of Extreme Behavioral Risk Management (XBRM), spoke at a well-attended workplace violence seminar that we presented this past year in New York City. In his remarks, Steve made an excellent point that safety and security in the workplace are shared responsibilities, specifically that:

＊ Employees at every level can never be passive observers to their own safety.

＊ Awareness and confidence have a "force multiplier" effect improving overall organizational safety and security.

＊ Employees do not want to depend on others for their safety.

These points drive home the rationale for effective workplace violence prevention through employee engagement. However, it doesn't happen by itself. Making your organization safe from the broad range of potential behaviors and incidents begins with your skills in creating an aware, caring culture of engagement. We do that at AlliedBarton through a well-coordinated mix of programs that provide some real structure for the effort.

Our approach to employee engagement pays off in two ways: When people feel fully invested in their company, with the knowledge that their leadership listens to them and cares, they're more likely to step up and say something when they observe troubling behavior. It also happens to enhance business performance and results, which is good for everyone.

Engagement and Security

The two goals, employee engagement and workplace security, are tightly intertwined. Just consider this: When workplace violence is reported, you frequently hear that the perpetrator was "isolated" or "disengaged." For incidents where workplace violence is perpetrated by someone from within the organization, that factor can be very critical indeed, since there likely would have been opportunities to engage that person. Engaged employees are going to be more inclined to point out issues, and more prone to jump in and help with a developing situation.

At AlliedBarton we have focused on creating an engagement culture that promotes constant development. This culture encourages employees who may start their career at an entry-level position and work their way up through the company with the support of the organization. It is important that every employee recognize the opportunity to advance his or her personal fulfillment, professional skills and connectedness with colleagues in the organization, so we work hard to ensure that development and engagement opportunities are available for everyone.

The challenge in all this lies in creating and nurturing a culture that reinforces the notion that there are no limits to what can be accomplished if you take full advantage of the available opportunities.

The Perils of Low Engagement

A lack of highly engaged employees can come back to haunt you in the event of a workplace violence threat. At the very least, it makes you less safe. A nationwide scientific survey we conducted in May 2011 provides strong

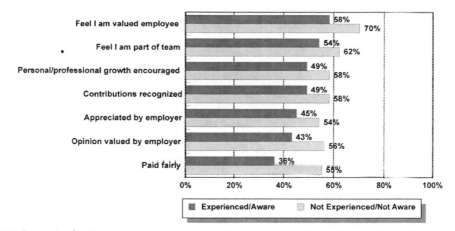

Workers who feel less engaged appear to witness more incidents of workplace violence in their organization.

evidence of a direct correlation between lower feelings of engagement and more workplace violence, as indicated in the table shown above. This data shows that in situations where only 58 percent of respondents reported that they feel valued by their employer, there is more observed workplace violence than in environments where 70 percent reported that they feel valued. In other words, the higher the feeling of engagement, the less violence. We also measured other aspects of employees' sense of how their companies value them, and in every case, there was less workplace violence when feelings of engagement and sense of worth were higher.

Leaders Are Showing Low Involvement

How do leaders of organizations respond when troubling behavior or outright violence is reported? Well, they appear reluctant to take any kind of aggressive action. The most likely type of action taken, according to our survey, is meeting with employees. About three in four (73 percent) of workers who witnessed, heard about or experienced workplace violence report that their employer held an employee meeting, and 69 percent say the employer met with the employee who experienced workplace violence.

However, only 45 percent of those employers implemented training programs for employees, and only 35 percent did so for supervisors. Changes to company policies were even less common, occurring only 22 percent of the time. Increasing security through the involvement of police or other authorities or contracting with a security agency were the actions least likely to be taken as a result of workplace violence. Probably as a result of this, fewer

than half (44 percent) of senior managers (CEO/president/owner) are perceived as being concerned with workplace violence, with only 17 percent
seen as being "very concerned" about the issue.

This all amounts to a low level of involvement by senior managers when
these events occur—essentially reflecting disengagement from the employee
base and their safety.

The Flip Side: When Employees are Engaged

In my experience, engaged employees consistently show superior performance in carrying out their duties. Obviously, in our business that translates
immediately to safety and protection for the lives, property and assets of our
clients. We have a monthly company newsletter, titled *The GREAT News*,
which spotlights outstanding employees and customer commendations.
The employees featured on its pages are shining examples of engagement in
action. Here are two examples:

- **Foiling unlawful access to a secure facility:** An AlliedBarton account
  manager and security supervisor prevented two suspicious individuals
  from gaining access under false pretenses to a client's Massachusetts
  facility. Two intruders presented themselves as employees of an environmental protection agency. When asked for credentials, they were
  unable to provide them. After attempting to verify the identity of the
  two individuals, our people discovered that they were not working for
  the agency and were not authorized to enter the facility. Nevertheless,
  the would-be trespassers made several unsuccessful attempts to enter
  the property. The quick thinking and leadership actions of our team
  prevented a breach of security.

- **On-the-job heroism:** In downtown Atlanta, a male was following a
  female in front of a client's facility. As the female was approaching the
  building, the male grabbed the female in a bear hug. A site supervisor
  and security officer witnessed the action from inside the lobby. They
  immediately ran to her aid, scaring the suspect away. They brought
  her inside the building and away from danger, and immediately called
  for police and waited until they arrived. Because a good description
  of the suspect and the direction he fled was provided, the police were
  able to apprehend him. In a letter of thanks, the victim touted the two
  security professionals as heroes.

Engagement and Execution

Of course, employee engagement not only keeps you safer but also furthers the organization's success overall. Outstanding companies recognize that excellent execution is the result of fully engaged employees. An organization's people define its character, affect its capacity to perform, represent the brand to the marketplace and reinforce its critical internal culture.

Japan is an outstanding example of how an engaged business culture and social environment can lead to greatness. It's a place where from birth parents are extremely focused in fostering a sense of engagement and self-worth in their children—so much so that whether you are laying bricks or are a top financial person or engineer, you take great pride in what you do.

After 2011's tsunami and subsequent nuclear crisis in Japan, I was very moved upon hearing of the people toiling in the extremely hazardous environment of the crippled power plant. I said to my family, "Do you know what heroes these people are? They're taking risk for others that may result in their getting sick and never going home again. They know that they're risking their lives to protect others." And it's amazing how the leadership culture in that society has resulted in such an exemplary level of performance and accountability to peers. It's unbelievable what those people have done.

We've taken that same attitude to heart here with effective, innovative and strategic human capital management approaches that serve as the cornerstone for us to accomplish both our business and our workplace safety goals. Managers at all levels actively support these concepts and are prepared and held accountable for effectively engaging our people.

Creating an Engagement Culture

If like me you feel your employees are your most valuable asset, and you do care about them, then you have to show them that they are valued. To achieve this goal you need to create an engagement culture while providing the tools for them to further their careers.

An engagement culture rests on open, proactive communication between management and the employee base, and also promotes constant personal and professional development. This encourages everyone to work their way up through the company with the support of the organization. Those who have advanced to management or executive positions are encouraged to reach out and help others do the same. This entire process strengthens the bonds of the organizational community and better prepares those in it for effectively dealing with any workplace violence issues that may arise.

This is why we offer a range of development programs that help build a foundation for employees to take a more proactive role in the company and hopefully advance through its ranks while doing so. The tools we provide for employee engagement and development include the following:

* The *Dare to be GREAT* Blueprint for Success value statement, which outlines our core values and philosophy pertaining to leadership, vision and teamwork.

* Our *GREAT News!* monthly company newsletter, where outstanding employee actions are showcased.

* A website, MyAlliedBarton.com, where employees can access important and timely information as well as connect with other teams across the country.

* The AlliedBarton EDGE®, our professionally designed and executed approach to training and development that includes hundreds of professional improvement courses.

* Other tools, such as an online employee suggestion box, employee surveys and next/best practices committees.

These programs reflect our core values of Growth, Responsibility, Empowerment, Achievement and Trust, hence the acronym GREAT.

Non-Negotiables for Operational Employees

When we created our *Dare to be GREAT* value statement, we hired a third-party firm to conduct online and in-person focus groups. We didn't survey all 50,000 people in the company, but we did reach thousands of employees, enough to validate the results. The data was evaluated and processed with the help of a strategic-planning specialist, and this essential booklet was the result. It prominently features "non-negotiables" for both management and operational employees, which we believe are essential to the success and viability of AlliedBarton. They reflect our commitment to our clients, employees and to each other. The employee non-negotiables include:

* **Ethics and Integrity:** All employees conduct themselves in an honest, ethical, professional manner.

* **Hiring Standards:** All employees are properly screened and licensed.

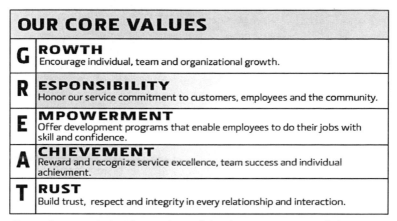

OUR CORE VALUES	
G	**ROWTH** Encourage individual, team and organizational growth.
R	**ESPONSIBILITY** Honor our service commitment to customers, employees and the community.
E	**MPOWERMENT** Offer development programs that enable employees to do their jobs with skill and confidence.
A	**CHIEVEMENT** Reward and recognize service excellence, team success and individual achievment.
T	**RUST** Build trust, respect and integrity in every relationship and interaction.

Core values coupled with coordinated development programs help to create a culture of employee engagement.

✦ **Training Standards:** All employees meet training standards and requirements and are able to professionally perform their duties.

✦ **Employee Relations:** All employees are treated respectfully and managed appropriately.

✦ **Employee Pay:** All employees are paid accurately and on time.

✦ **Billing:** All customers are billed accurately and on time.

✦ **Contract Compliance:** All contracts will be managed according to company and customer requirements.

These are solid principles by which to live and work, and are instrumental in fostering that important engagement culture. They certainly work for us.

ROUNDTABLE
Employee Awareness and Engagement

Bill Whitmore, *Chairman & CEO, AlliedBarton Security Services*
Rich Cordivari, *Vice President, National Accounts, AlliedBarton Security Services*
Bonnie Michelman, *Director of Police and Outside Services, Massachusetts General Hospital*
Patrick J. Wolfe, *former Vice President for Corporate Security, CIGNA Corporation, retired U.S. Secret Service*

Bill Whitmore: The concept of engagement works on many levels. Highly engaged companies produce better customer relationships. Highly engaged employees produce better employees. So that's our focus. Forget for a moment about the term "workplace violence." Is there a way to get people to start thinking about engagement—and projecting a caring attitude?

Bonnie Michelman: I think that we have two tough challenges: showing the connection between employee engagement and workplace violence prevention, and how do you make workplace violence everyone's job? If you do those two things well, then you've got an effective message of prevention.

Rich Cordivari: That's an interesting point. At a workplace violence session in the northeast a couple of weeks ago, a woman stood up during the Q&A and said, "One of my issues is that I have 400 or 500 employees and I have close to two dozen individuals who are 'inadvertent stalkers.' And everybody stopped and asked "What is that?" She went on to say that she worked in high tech and that the interpersonal skills of many employees are so bad that they literally don't understand that they are stalking women at work, or at least making them feel very uncomfortable. They don't even understand their own behavior; they think they are trying to start a relationship. She said this is a day-in and day-out issue, which I think really surprised others attending, and seems to relate to employee awareness and engagement. These young men have interpersonal skills that are so bad they are exposing the company to risk.

Whitmore: But what is their actual behavior?

Cordivari: She described them as "just nerdy to the nth degree." They would start hanging around a woman's desk after an initial and very casual interaction. They honestly don't get that they're not "dating" after one friendly conversation.

Whitmore: If you establish a culture of engagement, when the leaders say "We don't put up with that, we don't put up with discrimination, we don't put up with harassment—we are not going to stand for it. If you do it, you're gone." What's the cost of those call outs? Also, if you are running a production facility or call center—if you are getting people saying "Why do I need to take all these training programs—nobody cares around here."

Wolfe: The corporate executives will tell you that the corporation has tremendous values—respects people, a lot of diversity, no violence. When we tried to dismiss someone for violations of core values, the attorneys would become very uneasy counting on performance evaluations and not recognizing that those corporate values are themselves performance issues.

Michelman: We should all do what Tom Peters says: "Hire for attitude, not for skills."

Setting an Example

I am personally committed to participating in several business and management courses through Harvard Business Publishing this year, and have invited everyone on my management team to do likewise. That's because I believe that we need to set an example.

Organizations that value their employees at all levels ensure that development opportunities are available for them. Our front-line employees and security officers complete voluntary training because they want to increase their knowledge and further their careers. I get further into the topic of encouraging individual growth in Chapter 7.

Standing Committees

If you don't give employees a voice in the direction of the company, your chances of getting them to buy into what you are saying go down, and that factor increases exponentially when you're dealing with a company of 50,000 people.

This involvement is the type of reward that pays dividends for organizational health and security. It's not about somebody getting a pat on the back, but is far deeper than that. Here is an example: We have standing committees in the company. They could be on anything, be it risk, sales and marketing, technology. We rotate membership and invite managers to participate. Now put yourself in the position of your employees. If you believe that your organization really values your input, you feel like you're truly creating value—not necessarily monetary value, but a good customer relationship, a good employee touch.

The Safety Committee

Our division presidents, Ron Rabena and Randy Dorn, co-chair a company-wide safety committee that provides ongoing assessment and review of our own safety performance and culture. One of its flagship programs, Dare to be Safe, reinforces the importance of a safety-conscious work environment, with zero tolerance for avoidable injuries. It also ensures that all of our employees understand safety obligations and do what is necessary to fulfill their responsibilities.

To deliver the components of the program to all of our company's more than 100 offices, we've named a safety champion for each region, and safety messages are communicated through a calendar, monthly tips and an employee safety tool kit.

Employee Recognition

The way I see it, there are two levels of employee recognition. Of course there are the tangible rewards, such as financial compensation, but what I think really drives employees to excel is the intangibles that flow from a feeling of achievement. Here I'm not referring to simple pats on the back or applauding someone at the quarterly all-company meeting. It's more about reward by engagement. The more an employee shows a willingness to work toward your company's goals and objectives, the more that person should be involved in steering the company.

As the CEO, I get up every day and can't wait to go to work. I care about the employees of the company and strive to constantly demonstrate that through my actions, as well as through the many programs we offer to help them become more engaged and grow into a new crop of leaders.

As already mentioned one of the many things we do is to feature stories of employee accomplishment in every monthly issue of our company newsletter, *The GREAT News*, from customer commendations to on-the-job heroics and volunteer work on the part of employees that make life easier and more hopeful for the disadvantaged.

We've measured our employees' level of engagement on a continual basis by conducting pilot surveys at our field offices in various markets —an initiative we hope to develop further. This gives our management a sense of how connected our employees really feel. Low scores in a given market means that market gets more attention from headquarters. High scores will also make management sit up and take notice. If we come back in a market where employees already feel extremely engaged, we will take those managers and then help them mentor others. It's a combination of hiring people, giving them the tools, programs and practices to keep people engaged. That's powerful.

Other Improvement Programs

Engagement and advancement are also key themes in other areas of management and employee development as well, and we offer a range of employee improvement programs that I discuss in more detail in Chapter 7. For example, in 2010 we partnered with the University of Phoenix to offer tuition reduction to employees and college credit for the Master Security Officer (MSO) and New Recruiter Training Curriculum, a system that is built to recognize small gains and reward larger milestones. This also has been hugely popular, motivating thousands of our officers to invest their own time to improve themselves.

Clearly, developing of an engagement culture has become visible in every aspect of our company's business. In this sense we really are a learning organization—and that ethos is engrained as both a philosophy and as a broad toolset of courses and other structured personal and professional growth opportunities that are available to every one of our employees. I talk more about this in the next chapter on nurturing employee engagement.

With a solid foundation and a fully engaged team of professionals in place, the stage will be set for you to meet and exceed your goals, while making your organization safer. The course we have charted at AlliedBarton certainly is dependent on every member taking ownership of that concept.

Engagement Equals Good Defense

Sometimes workplace violence can occur despite the best efforts of coworkers and the organization. However, with strong employee engagement you will be better protected. A range of engagement and recognition policies, accompanied by the kinds of learning opportunities I cover in the next chapter, will place you in a much stronger position to ensure an informed, "see something, say something" culture.

Workplace violence awareness and prevention isn't a matter of simply announcing a policy or having your employees sign agreements. The typical climate of denial I discuss in Chapters 2 and 3 makes it necessary for you to mount an ongoing, concerted effort to shape the attitudes and culture of your organization. As we've done with many of our standing committees, you should encourage employee participation in the process of instilling and nurturing an engagement culture that protects everyone. It is also important that employees understand that they will be supported in their ongoing efforts of engagement and, when necessary, intervention in a troubling situation.

Training to raise awareness of the warning signs of workplace violence is key, as is the necessity to make sure employees understand their roles and responsibilities in the overall effort, and the specific steps they should take—the specific processes and tools at their disposal—should there be an incident to report or unusual behavior to evaluate.

Ultimately, educating, engaging and empowering every employee to observe and act is an essential key to your security. In the next two chapters I delve a bit further into how I see the attributes, processes and benefits of employee involvement and growth, and how that relates to organizational success.

GUEST EXPERT
Engaging Our Most Valuable Resource

By Jim Gillece, Chief People Officer, Senior Vice President, Human Capital Management, AlliedBarton

At AlliedBarton we look at people as our most valuable resource, hence my department's broad mission, which includes learning and development, organizational effectiveness, human resources, compensation, benefits and recruitment.

A major part of our efforts are focused on employee engagement, which pays huge dividends for the organization and its safety. Too often a company may be guided by the point of view of a very small minority. Continuing to rely on the same viewpoints over time, without giving the opportunity to others to voice ideas, is exclusionary. The cost of that exclusion is lost human capital and even alienation. If the best idea does not surface, the business will suffer: productivity and engagement will drop and talent will leave the organization, while poor morale and a "Why should I care" attitude ensues among those who are left. This "human exclusion cycle" is powerful and can be contagious if not treated.

I define my job as looking out for the future of our employees in the people pipeline. I remember that after my first promotion to a management position, my father told me "Congratulations, you are now the topic of dinnertime conversation." That got me thinking, and I quickly came to the conclusion that managers in effect serve the employees who directly report to them, and therefore should care about what is said about them at dinnertime conversations.

Take a minute to think about how your employees might answer the following questions: Does your boss care about you? Does your boss look out for your best interests? Are you being challenged?

Do you know what your next job is? Do you know how to get to that next job? If the answer to some of these questions is "no," you potentially have to make a "leadership adjustment" or begin to have some courageous conversations with people.

A manager is what I call the "Chief Climate Officer." There are macro events such as the economy and layoffs that can really rock cultures and create a lot of anxiety among employees. That anxiety then comes home as people interact with their spouses or become worried about their jobs, or deal with additional outlying factors that result in employees coming to work in a disjointed state of mind.

Having a manager who knows the employee, his or her personality, and recognizes a red flag or something unusual, is invaluable. This practice can entail reading a person's body language, a facial gesture, the tone of voice or the tone of an email. Managers have to be attuned to these things.

Good communication is key, and I believe that everyone has the ability—with proper practice and coaching—to improve the way they communicate. It's a skill that can always be further refined, and needs to be upgraded as a manager advances in his or her career. How well do you send and receive communications?

My personal favorite communications skill is the "Door Opener." In in a meeting, if I find someone who is being very quiet, I might say to that person, "Julie, I would like to hear some of your thinking on this subject as I bet you have a few good ideas." Chances are good she will not respond with "I have no ideas to offer." Being proactive to opening and unlocking the inclusion door sends the signal to that team member to please join our conversation and bring your best thoughts.

Engaged employees yield not only a more successful organization, but also one that is safer. You can correlate it to a winning sports team. When everyone on a team feels that he or she is contributing, everything is good. Players aren't bickering or fighting. If you have engaged employees who are creating great performance for your organization, that in turn creates opportunities where people can be the best they can be, putting their ideas to work in creating an even better working environment. This must certainly work to some degree to blunt the likelihood of workplace violence. And, in this type of culture, you're probably finding very good leadership.

Our leadership processes continues to teach leaders to tap the different, important and competitively relevant knowledge of their employees in order to foster enhanced business results and a sense of investment for all. We want to ensure that everyone here—from the top leadership to every employee at every desk—is learning, communicating and engaging to create a climate that enables everyone to grow, reach their greatest potential, and help keep our company healthy.

chapter 7

Encourage Individual Growth

If you value a safe and secure work environment, you need to spend the time, effort and resources to be sure that every employee has the very best opportunity to reach his or her full potential. This is about building intra-personal skills, where all people have a chance to look inside to see how they're doing, and then make changes to improve themselves.

Every year the American Psychological Association gives out awards for organizations that are found to be superior in their programs and practices for employee growth and development, engagement, work-life balance, recognition and other factors which lead to a healthy, secure workplace. The organizations that won this award most recently reported an employee turnover rate of just 11 percent, compared with a 38 percent national average. These organizations also found half as many employees reporting chronic work stress as compared to the national average (18 percent vs. 36 percent). The number of employees looking elsewhere for employment is only six percent in these workplaces as compared with 32 percent in the average work environment, with an overall job satisfaction rate of 87 percent! These statistics speak for themselves, with employee growth opportunities yielding lower turnover costs and a better bottom line.

For an organization such as ours, the opportunity for employee growth takes on additional value.

Many of our front-line people—those who work as security officers at job sites around the country—come from a lower socio-economic background. Often they've been beaten down in their lives to the extent that they haven't been able to hone strong job skills. To address that issue—to get to the point where the individuals who work for an organization are humming along—they need to feel safe and secure so that they're able to reach that level of self-actualization as articulated by Maslow.

So, we offer our employees every opportunity to improve themselves both personally and professionally. This makes them more productive, more invested and engaged in our organization and more satisfied with their work experience and the long-term prospects for their success. That all adds up to a more stable, safer workforce.

We see this focus on individual growth as a fundamental corporate value. We value a safe and secure work environment, and we're going to spend the time, effort and money to make sure everyone reaches their full potential.

Growth and Awareness: The Big Picture

I've been with AlliedBarton for 30 years, and from the early stages we always believed that training was going to be the basis of everything we do. Whether someone is a security officer working in a college dormitory or a payroll person working in one of our corporate offices, we believe that his or her training and growth will be a central building block from which we all become more successful and secure. So, over time we've invested in developing programs, developing leadership systems and, holding people to be accountable while making a full commitment to their training and development.

The opportunity to train and develop the people we recruit into this company is also important to me because it improves their lives, regardless of whether they stay with us for a long period of time or move on to do other things. It's a unique opportunity, and we've been effective in doing it. Developing these employees is our company's "higher calling." If we don't train and develop and give hope for our people to succeed and do better, and show them that we care about them, then I think we've failed. We've been a very successful company and I do believe our dedication to our employees' training and welfare is at the core of it.

I am really proud that our culture is driven by the phrase "Dare to be GREAT." To some people, those words may imply that we are bragging, but that's not what they are about at all. They are a challenge to be great. In a short period of time 40,000 of our 54,000 security officers have gone online, on their own time, and have signed up for that challenge.

Central to the values espoused in Dare to be GREAT, the multiple learning programs we offer comprise our ongoing effort to foster employee awareness and create a supportive environment. After all, if you don't have an environment where you can step up and help people, you may have a problem.

Becoming a Learning Organization

Giving your employees the opportunity to constantly grow, both professionally and personally, is an important aspect of creating a secure organization. I have proudly referred to AlliedBarton as a training organization for years. However, it became clear to me early on that the conventional training organization paradigm, which consists of the transfer of knowledge from an instructor to a learner, is no longer as effective as it once was. That's because delivering information in a standardized way to employees fails to prepare workers for their ever-changing roles.

The road to becoming a learning organization is no easy task, and that's due to constant change. Let's face it: we live in a much different world today than even five years ago. A learning organization simplifies the growth of its members by continuously transforming itself to meet the requirements of today's reality. With the pressures faced by modern companies that want to remain competitive in today's demanding business climate, I believe that the conventional training model needs to be shifted to a learning paradigm. As a learning organization, we are now able to address development opportunities in all facets of our business and are continually looking ahead to make sure everyone is taking advantage of the key learning tools that are important to their individual careers.

We've advanced the level of training for our personnel in three ways:

1. We have brought individuals with extensive training and development capability into the company.

2. We have listened to our customers and have developed training programs that can be broadly applied or are geared toward specific disciplines, such as those focused on serving the healthcare and higher education industries.

3. We use technology to drive these programs to make them readily available to our employees across the entire spectrum of the organization. Considering that we have more than 100 offices across the country and many of our employees work at client sites or company offices at any and all hours of the day, that factor becomes very important.

The development of a true learning culture has become visible in every aspect of our business. Whether it is a natural disaster that requires the actions of many and a coordinated team effort, or a solitary security officer on patrol at a mall who administers CPR on a customer, I see the result of a culture of learning in the proactive performance and positive attitude of the officers and managers in my company.

Immersion in a culture that promotes constant development encourages employees who may start "standing post" at an entry-level position to work their way up through the company with the support of the organization. Those who have worked their way up to management or executive positions are encouraged to reach out and help others do the same. Learning organizations ensure that development opportunities are available for employees at all levels. The company's front-line employees and security officers complete voluntary training because they want to increase their knowledge and further their careers.

Setting the standard in creating a true learning organization is especially important in the security business, since ongoing training enhances both safety and success. According to the Freedonia Group, the number of officers employed by private security firms is expected to increase 2.6 percent per year to 740,000 in 2014.

However, learning is critical to developing employees in any industry— those who can grow with the company, respond to unexpected challenges and step up to take proactive action should they observe any of the early warning signs of workplace violence. Learning organizations engage and empower employees not only to be competitive in 21st century society, but also to work in concert with their peers to keep us on an even keel, stepping in as a friend or an aware colleague when something seems not quite right.

All of these considerations have required us to remain intently focused on developing an innovative and secure culture based on leadership and employee development, with nationally recognized results. In 2010 we earned recognition as one of *Training* magazine's Top 125 training companies, the seventh consecutive year we attained that honor. Additionally, we were selected by *Chief Learning Officer* magazine as a LearningElite company. I'm proud of those recognitions.

ROUNDTABLE
Training for Workplace Violence Awareness

Bill Whitmore, *Chairman & CEO, AlliedBarton Security Services*
Rich Cordivari, *Vice President, National Accounts, AlliedBarton Security Services*
Chris Swecker, *former Assistant Director, Criminal Investigative Division, FBI*
Bonnie Michelman, *Director of Police and Outside Services, Massachusetts General Hospital*
Maureen Rush, *Vice President for Public Safety, University of Pennsylvania*
Patrick J. Wolfe, *former Vice President for Corporate Security, Cigna Corporation, retired U.S. Secret Service*

Rich Cordivari: One of our goals today was to bring people in with a point of view around this topic and especially from some of the vertical markets that we serve where we think there is a particular challenge to get significant points of view—not only to train our employees, but also to inform us so that we can do a better job getting that message out through awareness and education programs. So how does training fit into all of this?

Bill Whitmore: If you look at a pie chart on all losses resulting from injuries in the workplace, I think number one is traffic accidents; number two is accidents with equipment, and number three is workplace violence. I've worked with companies that saw the value in training every employee who ever drove a vehicle, or a program for everyone who drove a forklift, before they could get on it because they didn't want incidents that damaged the product or hit other people. There are all kinds of training about using equipment such as cars or forklifts. But there seems to be a disconnect with the number three item on the list. Why doesn't workplace violence prevention get the same level of training attention?

Cordivari: When you look at some of these areas that Bill mentioned, it's easy to understand what they are. The behaviors that will help one to improve are obviously coachable. I can teach you to drive better, I can teach you how to operate a forklift better or I can teach you to use a particular piece of equipment better. However, with workplace violence prevention, we are talking about emotional issues attached to all of the influences that employees bring into the workplace day-to-day; and you just can't put your finger on it. It's all human behavior.

Bonnie Michelman: You've heard of "zero tolerance." Well, in my organization, I use that expression because I think that really is the case. You have to think about how to prioritize this concept in people's minds, so that the way you do everything else is not discrete or ignorant to best practices for prevention. That's very hard for people to capture. It not as clear; it's more amorphous.

Whitmore: Should identification and intervention be part of a management curriculum? Should it be part of training for every new manager?

Chris Swecker: At one of my companies we tried to get it incorporated into some of our new employee training and it was a constant battle competing for time—competing for employee time and even customer time.

Whitmore: After a workplace violence event, how do the results of the debriefing sessions find their way back into the organization so that change can be created? How do we communicate with the people who are in charge of training our employees to do the things you found out about? I know it differs by organization.

Maureen Rush: Whatever we write down in the after action report about what we thought should be done differently, a major sporting event like Penn relays, for example, we make sure when the detail is created the next year those points are brought over. So it is incorporated into the future plans of the event.

Cordivari: How are lessons of civil treatment learned? How do you foster an awareness of the importance of civil treatment that drives corporate cultures from the bottom, so that people coming in the door know on day one that they are in a culture where a) their safety is valued and b) that if they see something they can step up and say something, and action will be taken?

Patrick J. Wolfe: That was the value at CIGNA and the value of the HR division. It is a standard at the company and has been for at least 10 years. A new employee comes in, and they get it right away. These are the principles of the company.

Whitmore: A person I respect in our business believes that the people who are on the ground are often the ones who don't get enough training and don't understand the issues—and they are in the trenches every day. So, he works with the HR leaders who handle that issue. HR is on the ground level with the worker, and he believes that has made a difference. This is often an HR issue.

Michelman: A lot of companies make it part of their performance appraisals.

Wolfe: That's how it is drilled down—through the performance evaluations. That's best practice.

Training Programs

At AlliedBarton we hold managers at every level accountable for developing their people. This leads to both high retention and better morale—key factors in making our organization highly effective and a less likely venue for any kind of workplace violence incident.

Our approach to professional and personal development is designed to make sure that our employees are prepared to excel at their current positions and to prepare them to take on additional responsibilities and authority in the future. This is consistent with our commitment to keep people for a long time, develop and foster their investment in our company and its safety, and put them in the best possible position to lead this organization in the future.

Individual growth begins when a new employee receives a copy of our *Dare to be GREAT Blueprint for Success*. As a value statement, it serves the following purposes:

- It outlines core values and philosophy pertaining to leadership, vision and teamwork.

- It highlights the core purpose of our organization, to serve and secure the people, homes and businesses of our communities.

- It details our ideal culture and provides management, operational and security officer mandates that we all live by.

- It highlights critical characteristics and attributes that we demand of our employees to be successful and achieve greatness.

This activity is just the beginning of an extended growth path for our employees. It continues with our learning paths, performance management systems, mentorships and recognition programs. All are designed to support and cultivate leaders at all levels of the company.

Our employee website, MyAlliedBarton.com, offers a sustainable method of employee communication to engage our professionals in a way previously unseen in the security industry, and probably in a lot of other sectors as well. This site is where all employees can access important and timely information as well as connect with other teams across the country.

AlliedBarton's approach to employee development is illustrated in the following chart. At each "turn" on the development ladder there are formal processes for making sure that each employee fully understands his or her

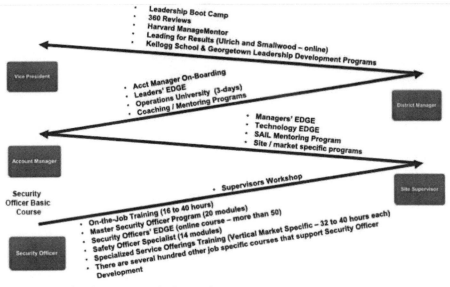

AlliedBarton development tracks for employees.

role in that new position and has immediate access to the tools and people who will act as mentors on their new path.

AlliedBarton EDGE

Our entire learning organization is centered on AlliedBarton EDGE (Educate, Develop, Grow and Engage), a professionally designed and executed approach to training and development that includes e-learning through an enhanced learning management system. This program begins with the recruiting and screening process for all levels and extends throughout the organization to include officers, managers, executives and support staff.

Web-based training enables our employees to complete modules at their own pace and schedule. Tracking and compliance functionality enables managers to verify course completion and ensure that new and existing teams are properly trained and prepared for their planned duties as well as the unexpected. Leadership topics are present throughout, and there are training modules specific to leadership.

Prior to the launch of the EDGE in early 2009 our employees typically completed about 10,000 courses online each year. In 2010 our employees completed more than 600,000 AlliedBarton EDGE online training courses, which is extremely gratifying to me and gives me confidence that we have a strong, vibrant organization.

Growth for Managers

Because I'm the CEO of the company you might think I believe I am well trained, but there's always room for growth at any level, so I'm actually enrolled in the EDGE program myself, taking a series of managerial courses called ManageMentor, provided by Harvard Business Publishing. These are readily available to anyone from front-line management up to my level in the company. EDGE courses at this level include:

* Budgeting
* Coaching
* Decision Making
* Developing Employees
* Diversity
* Finance Essentials
* Goal Setting
* Leading and Motivating
* Marketing Essentials
* Negotiating
* Strategic Thinking
* Strategy Execution
* Team Leadership
* Team Management
* Time Management

Despite objections from some that the CEO shouldn't be spending his valuable time taking online courses, I firmly believe that it's vitally important that everyone participate, and I'm no exception. After all, if I don't hold myself accountable to it, how can I hold anybody else accountable? Additionally, every one of my direct reports has an objective to take 15 of these courses, and their participation determines part of their bonus.

We also offer a number of courses for general managerial skills, such as:

* **Supervisor's Workshop:** A one-day instructor-led course that covers effective supervision skills. All new site and shift supervisors are required to attend this course within 60 days of appointment to the position.

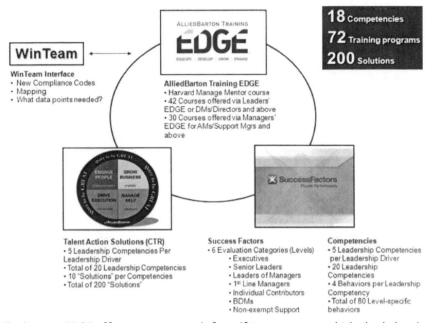

AlliedBarton EDGE offers numerous tools for self-improvement, which also helps the entire organization.

↠ **Operations University:** Helps new managers better understand AlliedBarton's business processes so that they can deliver high quality service to our customers. The course covers a wide variety of business and security-related topics.

Mentoring with SAIL

AlliedBarton encourages mentoring as a resource for identifying and developing individuals with the knowledge and skills to achieve our imperatives. Informal mentoring takes place from the very start of an employee's career. Introduced in 2008, SAIL (Security Academy in Leadership) includes formal meetings, training sessions and day-to-day interactions between mentors and protégés. Mentors/protégés are nominated by their leadership team. A contract is established to ensure that SAIL will generate tangible results. Initial results were very encouraging, with more than 65 employees entering SAIL in its initial weeks.

New mentoring programs continue to be deployed. At a recent leadership event we implemented a Peer Mentoring Network designed to provide career development tools. The objective of the network is to foster an inclusive, mentoring culture where colleagues are encouraged to select their advisers based on respect and recognition of expertise. The program was structured by encouraging participants to build a profile that included strengths and development opportunities. Participants matched themselves based on need. Sample agenda items include work/life balance, managing upward and overcoming obstacles.

Other Growth Programs

In 2010 we partnered with the University of Phoenix to offer both a tuition reduction to employees and college credit for any courses they may choose, as well as Master Security Officer (MSO) and New Recruiter Training Curriculum (NRTC). These opportunities not only serve as additional benefits to our employees who are furthering their education, but are a testament to the quality of our training and the extensive nature of our employees' preparation.

Our MSO training is a 20-module, self-paced program covering a range of security topics. Upon completion, employees achieve the coveted Allied-Barton Master Security Officer designation. The NRTC that focuses on quality versus quantity hiring, ensuring new hires meet AlliedBarton's rigorous security officer standards and the needs of each client.

We will continue to develop the best training in the security industry. Our leaders have embraced our belief that training and development are paramount to business success, personal development and team building. By enabling our employees to grow in this way, we further enhance our culture, values and beliefs with passion, and demonstrate the true meaning of leadership.

Measuring Performance Includes Communication

Throughout our entire range of learning opportunities we've embedded a performance management system, so we literally can look at every individual in the company to evaluate their training level and performance. We then combine this with MyAlliedBarton.com, where they can share information, training, news, opportunities and give us feedback.

Clear communication and articulation of what good performance looks like at different levels aligns development with measurable business goals, while making sure that managers are attuned to the personal concerns, and sometimes the troubles, of their employees. The performance management process and having very clear, defined competencies at each level helps everybody, including the employee, understand what "good" looks like.

This constant circle of training programs, feedback, manager-employee communication and continual improvement of the entire system is fostering growth and engagement, making our organizational community stronger, more productive and more secure.

Setting an Example

AlliedBarton's performance management system and performance reviews are closely tied to the company's leadership focus. In a recent issue of our employee newsletter, The GREAT News, our St. Louis District Manager Jerry Cassidy described his take on leadership, mentoring and how it makes our company stronger and safer.

"I believe strongly that if every leader focused their attention on taking care of their officers, the officers would take care of them and our clients," Jerry wrote. "From a structural standpoint, everyone needs a chain of command, someone to get answers from and someone to be a mentor. To take the steps to become a leader, the first step is to find the right mentor. You then have to raise your hand and identify yourself as a person who wants to move up and ask your mentor the steps to move into a leadership role and you will find yourself down the path to leadership."

Guy Hassfield, Vice President, National Accounts, is another Allied-Barton leader who has taken our training opportunities and run with them, becoming a recognized leader in the pages of The GREAT News, as well as in the organization overall. As Guy puts it, "Since joining AlliedBarton I have taken every opportunity to be mentored, both formally and informally, by those that I have worked with or to whom I have reported. There are tremendous amounts of learning opportunities available when you take advantage of the daily interactions that are both structured and unstructured with leaders in our company. I have never been tentative or reluctant to ask questions, I involve myself in additional work assignments and spend additional time with clients learning how their business works and what is important to their culture."

These are just two of the many, many examples we have of employees who have grown professionally as part of our company's learning culture, giving back along the way to further strengthen our safe and productive environment.

The Value of Growing

I've been with my company a long time, so I've heard this for years: You have to provide quality training and tools to allow people to be successful. As a professional you should never stop growing and learning. I don't care what level you are at the company. You constantly have to try to grow personally and learn. In our industry, things constantly change. Our internal and external customers have regulatory issues that evolve over time, and there are training programs that change. Like most industries, it's a dynamic environment—one in which we need to continually adapt so that we are able to exceed the demands of our clients.

But no matter what tools or what technologies you have, no matter how efficient and productive you are, you still have to have employees that are striving for results. At the end of the day it's all about the employees.

Organizations that create real leaders empower employees to be competitive in our 21st century society so they can continue to be relevant, challenged, engaged and productive. The training available to your own employees will create an incredible opportunity for their growth and development, both personally and professionally.

Providing employees at all levels with the opportunity to gain new skills yields multiple dividends. It not only increases the effectiveness with which they perform their duties, but also enhances the overall work experience, increasing motivation and job satisfaction, while helping them more effectively manage stress. All of this boosts your bottom line, makes your organization a happier and safer place to work, which in turn makes it more attractive to top talent, which multiplies the overall impact even further. That's why a learning culture should be key to your overall workplace violence prevention program.

GUEST EXPERT
Training and Technology

By Rich Cordivari, *Vice President, National Accounts; former Vice President, Learning & Development, AlliedBarton Security Services*

The digital revolution is transforming our culture and is clearly altering the way we communicate with each other. Nowhere is technology's power more visibly demonstrated than with training. In fact, the key to a successful training program for employees is to use technology as a tool for making learning opportunities flexible and accessible to all. The way we see it at AlliedBarton, training for entry-level employees is not enough. A true learning culture constantly focuses on learning and development and makes these opportunities available to all levels, in multiple formats, at all times.

As Vice President of Learning and Development, I have led AlliedBarton's team of learning professionals who deliver services to employees in more than 100 operating units. While classroom training is a crucial component of our programs, technology tools dramatically expand the horizon for each employee. Technology enhances learning in the following ways:

Motivation and Accessibility: Technology helps motivate learners because it allows them to access learning opportunities in a way that is immediate, convenient, and familiar. Someone in a remote region, for example, may have to wait to attend an in-person class while online training is available immediately. People may also be motivated and excited by the opportunity to participate in an activity that uses new and familiar technology.

- **Assessment Tools:** Technology tools offer the ability to measure the effectiveness of the programs offered. Are people learning and is this having a positive effect on their roles? Are the learning goals aligning with strategic goals?

- **Variety:** Internet training makes learning opportunities available in ways that provide flexibility for an organization and allow security personnel to learn a greater variety of relevant material in a timely manner.

- **Compliance:** Compliance requirements for certain companies and employees vary state by state and are subject to frequent change. With virtual training, updated modules can be easily and quickly added, which ensures that employees are up to speed on new industry, state and contractual client compliance requirements.

- **Productivity:** Essential functions such as payroll, billing, and other similar internal support processes can be delivered electronically, which frees up instructors to focus on those areas where face-to-face training is more effective.

→ **Career Mobility:** Knowledge is power and a fast-track for advancement awaits employees who tap into the digital domain for 24/7 training.

We currently offer more than 400 online programs that support 16 different learning paths. Our comprehensive online learning management system provides multiple platforms including the Security Officers' EDGE, Managers' EDGE and Leaders' EDGE. Employees log into the appropriate platform and complete a wide range of training modules. The system is interactive and easy to access, making learning and development opportunities available on demand. These learning opportunities result in better prepared and engaged security teams at customer sites.

E-learning, however, should not be a stand-alone program. Before initiating new e-learning programs in your organization, consider what role you want technology to play in your training programs and what might be missing in training and education programs in a machine-dominated age. As learning technologies become more sophisticated, so too must our critical assessments of their impact on our lives.

While online training has been adopted in a way that I find very gratifying, traditional classroom, face-to-face personal training will never go away. Having the advantage of being able to deliver courses online for broad issues and then have talented trainers address site-specific, state-specific, industry-specific issues in face-to-face classroom environments is the way we're able to ensure high quality and consistency.

chapter 8

Make Workplace Violence Prevention Everyone's Job

E veryone in your organization has a responsibility to be an active participant in trying to stop workplace violence before it happens. This means stepping up—showing leadership in observing odd or troubling behavior, suspicious persons or unusual activity and then doing something about it.

This sounds simple enough, but stepping up and calling someone out is a very difficult thing to do, as it runs counter to the common workplace culture where people tend to keep their heads down and focused on the job, creating as few waves as possible. Consequently, employees can't be expected to adopt this kind of attitude just because someone sends around a memo that says "See something, say something," although that is a start. To most effectively act on this motto, they need education, awareness and organizational support.

None of us can be passive observers to our own safety. Educating, engaging and empowering every employee to observe and then act is an essential key to your security.

Right in Front of Us

Workplace violence in its various forms is all too prevalent in the American business world, so it only makes sense that employees should be our first line of defense in combating it. Yet far too many American workers are not being fully engaged in workplace violence prevention.

I'll show you what I mean: The national workplace violence survey that AlliedBarton conducted in May 2011 found that more than half of Americans employed outside their homes (52 percent) have witnessed, are aware of or have experienced a violent event or an event that can lead to violence at their workplace. These events include open hostility, abusive language or threats and can escalate up to the infliction of significant physical harm to someone by another person.

Even more significant is that 28 percent of workers have actually experienced a violent event, or one that can lead to violence, at their current place of employment. (Overall, 12 percent have witnessed, heard about or are aware of an incidence of significant physical harm to another person and five percent have had this happen to them or have been personally affected by this type of incident.)

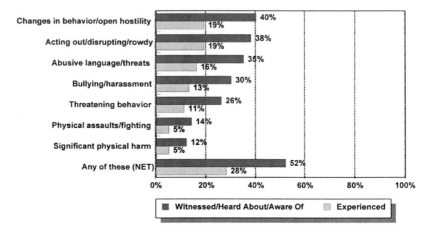

More than half of American workers have witnessed, heard about or have experienced workplace violence.

This high incidence of workplace violence and related events reflect significant level of concern with personal safety in the workplace. In fact, our survey found that about one in three (34 percent) of those Americans employed outside the home are "very" or "somewhat concerned" with their personal safety.

Nevertheless, these same workers are often reluctant to report incidents of violence and related events that occur at their place of employment. Even with the high levels of concern for their personal safety, nearly three in ten (29 percent) of those who have witnessed, heard about or experienced workplace violence did not report the incident or take any other actions. The most common action taken by employees was reporting the incident to their supervisor or human resources, with about two in three (62 percent) doing that.

Workers who experienced or are aware of violence are even less likely to take other actions when violence occurs at their place of employment. Twenty-one percent contacted security, 14 percent reported the incident to the police and 12 percent called a confidential number provided by their employer. This low level of reporting reflects that most incidents of workplace violence are mild (e.g., disruptive behavior, verbal abuse, bullying), and it is likely that many workers are not aware that this behavior can escalate into more serious events.

All of this clearly supports the necessity to get more employees—ideally all employees—more aware, connected and involved with securing their workplace. To not do so is simply accepting unnecessary risk.

Shared Responsibilities

Steven M. Crimando, Managing Director of Extreme Behavioral Risk Management (XBRM), a division of AllSector Technology Group, Inc., spoke at a well-attended workplace violence seminar that we presented this past year in New York City. Steve made a number of excellent observations about the concept that safety and security in the workplace are shared responsibilities. His talk included these points:

+ Employees at every level can never be passive observers to their own safety.

+ Awareness and confidence have a "force multiplier" effect for improving overall organizational safety and security.

+ Employees do not want to depend on others for their safety. In other words, they feel more comfortable when they are empowered to help ensure workplace security.

+ Behavior and communication remain the best predictors of violence.

+ You don't need to be a mental health professional to be concerned about troubling behaviors observed in workplace. Everyone—all employees—can be on the front lines of prevention.

Steve also discussed a well-established psychological principal, known as Lewin's Equation, which is expressed as $B = f(P,E)$—behavior is a function of the person and the environment. This means that when addressing

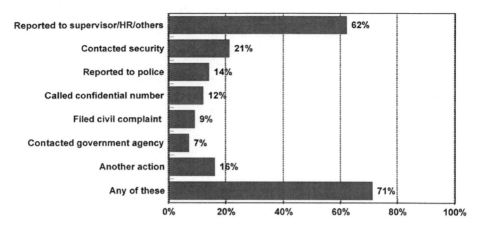

Employees take various actions as a result of workplace violence.

workplace violence prevention, we must consider aspects of the predictable personal behavior of our employees, the influence of the environment in which they're working, and the interaction between the two. This obviously calls for top-down attention to those factors of education, awareness and organizational support.

Action Binds Anxiety: Educating Employees

The person who coined the phrase "action binds anxiety" is Dr. Peter Sandman, a well-known risk communications specialist who is quoted regularly in the news media and often weighs in on people's stressors during different types of crises. His statement essentially means that people react better to dangerous or crisis situations when they are armed with actionable information. While Dr. Sandman's perspectives on risk communications address a wide variety of crisis situations, they also speak very specifically to workplace violence prevention and response.

Research shows that people actually benefit in a number of ways when management is very clear and accurate about both threats and remedies—not merely hinting about threats or keeping them hidden. Organizations achieve the best results when people are actually very aware of any risks that may face them, and that comes about when management clearly and honestly talks about threats of violence, what the organization is doing about them, what employees can and should do with regard to awareness and prevention, as well as the proper reaction when something does happen.

Crimando notes that usually there are two places where companies make mistakes in this regard:

- ➤ They downplay talking to employees about the hazards of workplace violence, minimizing or keeping it cloaked in some way.

- ➤ They address workplace violence and its prevention by suggesting a very limited and simple list of things that employees can do, such as reporting odd behavior, but leave out specific action-oriented steps.

This means that your organization will get the best results when you present to employees a balanced view of the workplace violence landscape —giving them complete information about any threat, but counterbalancing that with information about how the organization and they, as individuals, can actively reduce the threat or increase safety and survival. Demonstrate to your employees that your organization has a policy on workplace violence prevention, including specific, active programs and procedures, including exercises, for all stakeholders, from c-suite management to line workers. Doing so will create a "sweet spot" of employee empowerment and organizational safety.

Creating Awareness Among Employees

So how do you get your employees more involved in workplace violence prevention? This can be accomplished through formalized policies and programs focusing on awareness and informed threat assessment, promulgated from the top down at all levels of the organization. As I discuss throughout this book, it needs to be both pushed and embraced by leadership, with learning and awareness programs made available to employees at all levels.

Effective awareness education should include a thorough familiarization of the workplace violence continuum that appears in Chapter 1 of this book, with the goal of raising employee consciousness about the different levels of workplace violence and how to recognize them. This familiarization should begin with orientation when an employee is first hired, and should be followed by testing and periodic ongoing workshops to assure that understanding is fully absorbed. Involving a team or teams of employees from different disciplines can be a very effective approach to fostering employee involvement.

Your human resources department should take a leadership role in spreading the word on workplace violence recognition and managing related workshops. HR's efforts, in turn, should be visibly supported and trumpeted by management continually and at all levels—and not just through words, but actions. Management should be visible at workshops and training sessions whenever possible, while leaders taking workplace violence prevention training should be noted by the organization's employee newsletter.

Employee Awareness Topics

Workplace violence prevention training for employees should include the following topics, which already are followed widely in many government agencies:

+ The nature of the problem: Definitions and descriptions of what constitutes workplace violence

+ Your organization's workplace violence policy, which should reinforce the value of reporting behaviors or incidents, and the procedures for doing so

+ "Warning signs," "red flags" and other behavioral indicators of potential violence

+ Ways of dealing with hostile persons, including preventing or defusing volatile situations or aggressive behavior

+ Managing anger and conflict resolution skills

+ Stress management, relaxation techniques, wellness training

+ Security procedures, e.g., the location and operation of safety devices such as alarm systems

+ Basic emergency procedures, including who to call and what support resources and services are available

+ Personal security measures, including action steps to implement during a violent situation

Workplace violence often stems from a sense of injustice or unfairness. As previously mentioned, people do not simply snap. More often they ruminate and stew over their beliefs and feelings that they are not being heard or respected. Workplace violence is typically the product of smoldering anger, not sudden anger. Therefore, open-door programs administered by HR, including ombudspersons, alternative dispute resolution, and mediation, should be visible and available to assist employees in resolving conflicts. A confidential employee assistance program (EAP) can provide trained counselors who can address workplace stress and behavioral issues. You can use these counselors as a way to assess whether a situation needs to be brought to the attention of management, or even to strategize ways to deal with uncomfortable or threatening situations.

Pay special attention to general supervisory training, including the basic leadership skills I discuss in Chapter 5. Managers do not need to be workplace violence experts themselves, but certainly do need to know which experts to call. Again taking a cue from government, basic topics for managers should include the following:

* Skills in taking disciplinary actions
* Skills in handling crisis situations
* Skills in conflict resolution

Above all, managers at all levels should serve as role models for awareness and preparedness. Managers must also remember to deal with persons of concern with dignity and fairness. As individuals perceived to have the greatest degree of control in the workplace, managers and their conduct are a critical elements in inhibiting and facilitating violent behavior.

Threat Assessment

Our workplace violence continuum provides excellent guidance for anyone wishing to assess a potentially troubling situation. Unusual or disturbing behavior should always be treated seriously by reporting it in a manner consistent with the system you set up for your organization. Any report should in turn be evaluated by a threat assessment team or other appropriate company personnel, which could include the following organizational stakeholders:

* Management
* Employee relations personnel
* Employee assistance program personnel
* Law enforcement, and/or security
* Civil rights organizations
* Your safety and health management office
* Unions, where applicable
* Your conflict resolution team

The approach and timing for your threat assessment evaluation should be specific to the circumstances of the potentially violent situation. Once a threat assessment is completed, your in-house experts can decide what additional measures are needed to address any situation. As always, clear communication is critical. Management should explain to involved employees or others who may be affected what steps are being taken and why.

Hotlines and Emergency Plans

Any comprehensive employee program should include a hotline for reporting unusual behavior or potentially destructive situations, and that number should be constantly circulated with high visibility to your entire workforce

A crisis response plan should include clear steps on what to do should there be a violent incident. Your plan should be specific to the type of facility, building, and the workers it covers, and should describethe following procedures:

- Calling for help
- Calling for medical assistance
- Notifying the proper authorities or whoever is acting in their place, including security personnel and the police
- Learning emergency escape procedures and routes
- Finding safe places to escape inside and outside of the facility
- Securing the work area where the incident took place
- Accounting for all employees if a facility is evacuated
- Identifying personnel who may be called upon to perform medical or rescue duties
- Addressing psychological trauma resulting from a violent event

These are all guidelines recommended by government agencies and followed by hundreds of successful organizations. Of course, one size doesn't fit all, so you should feel free to customize any and all of these for your particular business, workforce, venue and other unique organizational attributes.

ROUNDTABLE
Making HR an Effective Partner in Prevention

Bill Whitmore, *Chairman & CEO, AlliedBarton Security Services*
Bonnie Michelman, *Director of Police and Outside Services, Massachusetts General Hospital*
Maureen Rush, *Vice President for Public Safety, University of Pennsylvania*
Patrick J. Wolfe, *former Vice President for Corporate Security, Cigna Corporation, retired U.S. Secret Service*

Bill Whitmore: Human Resources needs to be a key partner in preparing employees for workplace violence prevention and response.

Patrick J. Wolfe: However, here's an issue: There is a new model in the workplace, and instead of having one "generalist" HR person for every 150 or 200 people, it is now 1 to 1,000 or 1 to 1,200—someone who is not a workplace violence or security expert. That's the bad news. The good news is that organizations concerned about prevention of violence in the workplace are not just talking to the generalists anymore; they are talking to security. They are connected with people scattered around the United States regionally. They know who to contact, and that has proven to be very beneficial and efficient.

Maureen Rush: You've got to set the tone for workplace violence prevention and everyone's role in the beginning at new employee orientation, and throughout the HR on-boarding process. But how many organizations really focus on workplace violence prevention at that point? Is it mandatory? Does it get "watered down" because of time? You have to attend to all of the HR issues, including workplace violence prevention, from day one.

Whitmore: What about after the fact? What are next practices that could involve HR?

Rush: Something we haven't discussed is the new word being bandied about today—"CISM teams"—Critical Incident Stress Management Debriefing teams, where you bring in trained people from your organization after the incident. At that point, people are totally unproductive, they are afraid. Then in addition to telling them what happened you'd better be caring for them not only for today, but for months after with that CISM team. That's the big issue today. You are seeing more and more companies investing internally in CISM teams or hiring consultants from the outside.

Bonnie Michelman: What exacerbates a crisis is the rumor mill. You have to quell that immediately. The last thing you want to do is inflame rumors, so getting accurate information out quickly is critical. You have to put the incident in context for them, to make them realize this is one incident out of how many in the number of years and what you are doing about it.

Wolfe: We owned an employee assistance program (EAP) company, and we started sending out teams back in 1997. Now it's the hottest thing, so it was a good investment. If there is a workplace violence incident, the EAP has proved very beneficial in the aftermath. We also use the team when an employee has died unexpectedly.

Michelman: Here are the toughest points: First, what is the connection between employee engagement and workplace violence; and, how do you make workplace violence everyone's job? I think that really is the challenge, because if you do that well, you're able to disseminate your message of prevention.

Anticipating Employee Response to an Incident

When building your employee awareness and response programs, you need to account for human behavior, especially when gaging how employees will respond when a violent incident occurs. This factor often is overlooked or ridden with inaccurate assumptions. Steven Crimando routinely sees two major errors in incident response plans that he reviews.

"One is to not have any behavioral layer at all. And the other is that plans are based on flawed behavioral assumptions. Leaders and planners are not really trying to anticipate how people will behave in certain emergencies. They simply have a one-size-fits-all model," Crimando says. He notes that this typical flaw in planning is addressed in a study titled "Redefining Readiness: Terrorism Planning Through the Eyes of the Public" that was conducted in September 2004 by the New York Academy of Medicine. Its researcher and principal investigator was Dr. Roz D. Lasker.

"Lasker and her associates, through random phone dialing, surveyed a significant part of the population and asked them how they would respond to two terrorism scenarios—a dirty bomb and a small pox outbreak," Crimando explains. "She found that two-fifths of the American people would refuse to go to the vaccination site in the case of the smallpox outbreak, and only three quarters would seek shelter as instructed in the event of a dirty bomb explosion. What this reveals is the plans that are being built right now are destined to fail in major crisis events because we do not understand how the American public actually sees these emergencies."

Based on the detailed results of this study, Crimando believes that we can learn a few lessons about preparedness as it relates to human behavior. Specifically:

- → In the face of a serious threat you need to be very specific—how people react in hour one is different than how they react in day one, over the course of a month, or after a year. You have to be able to anticipate how behavior changes along a timeline—short and long term, and plan to address those changing behaviors.

- → People respond to specific hazards in different and specific ways. You don't react the same way to a shooter as you would to a disease outbreak or a bomb, and so on. You can't apply a one-size-fits-all model. You have to understand how to people behave in different threat scenarios and plan accordingly.

- → Some of our "emergencies" are primarily behavioral. In the wake of the 1995 sarin poison gas attack in the Tokyo subway system, responders experienced a huge number of victims that had all of the symptoms of gas poisoning, but hadn't actually been poisoned. In fact this event produced a 4:1 ratio of behavioral casualties to medical casualties. It was the huge psychological reaction that overwhelmed the government's response capabilities because authorities did not accurately anticipate what the behavior would look like in that type of emergency.

The point is this: If you don't pay careful attention to the lessons learned from different kinds of scenarios, you could be modeling something that is all wrong, and during the crisis event, it's going to leave you in a potentially fatal situation. It is critical to apply the lessons learned in other incidents because during a crisis the learning curve is way too steep.

Touching Every Level of the Organization

To ensure that workplace violence prevention is perceived as "everyone's job," a high level of awareness, including its risks, preventative measures and necessary responses, needs to saturate every level of the organization, from the CEO through middle management and every employee. Not having a comprehensive awareness program will create weak links among segments of your workforce.

At the c-suite, there is a whole range of concerns. People at that level will benefit from discussions that are not just about their fiduciary responsibilities, OSHA compliance or employment and liability issues. They also need to think about workplace violence case precedents, including different statutes from state to state and key cases that have formed our national posture on workplace violence.

Workplace violence awareness and preparation also needs to be extended to the perimeters of the workforce—from lone workers to mobile workers to those who may be working from home. For example, consider the scenario of a pharmaceutical sales representative and the drug addict up the block who knows what this representative does. The addict also knows that the representative's vehicle is loaded with samples, and that every day this person walks out of the house carrying a bag displaying the pharmaceutical company's logo. This salesperson certainly has some very unique threat risks, as do many other professionals. These special aspects always need to be carefully considered when crafting effective awareness and response programs.

The Importance of Practice

For employees at all levels, awareness means introducing and practicing specific skills. People will lose these skills if they don't get a chance to practice them, and without practice they are not going to effectively do the right things in a high-stress condition. So there is tremendous value in repetition in crisis-related behaviors that we want from our employees. This is another place where many employers fall short.

Very often people will have the sense that it is one thing to talk about workplace violence, but going beyond that to actually rehearse response plans may be too frightening. That's a fallacy. Everyone has rehearsed evacuating through routine, mandated fire drills, yet most organizations have never rehearsed shelter places or hideouts, and certainly most have never introduced any idea of what would it would mean to fight back in the event of a violent event. That needs to change.

I recommend following the OSHA perspective of understanding hazards, understand the defense, and the importance of acting in time when trouble hits the fan. It's kind of like muscle memory—employees must be trained to almost instinctively and automatically react in the proper manner.

That's why we do fire drills, because if there is a real fire we go on autopilot to get out of that environment. Very few employers have gone to that level with workplace violence issues, but that's the way to strengthen your response capabilities—with practice and repetition.

 Psychological First Aid

By Steven M. Crimando, *Managing Director, Extreme Behavioral Risk Management, a division of AllSector Technology Group, Inc.*

During a violent or threatening event, or in its immediate wake, there can often be a significant delay in accessing higher levels of medical care or psychological support. Just as victims of a violent workplace incident may require medical first aid, the survivors of a violent attack also urgently need psychological first aid (PFA) to give them the best chance for rebounding and coping with the emotional consequences of the experience in the weeks and months ahead.

The first hours and days after a violent incident are a critical window for psychological intervention. In a growing body of research exploring the neuro-circuitry of extreme fear and the neuro-chemistry of traumatic stress, scientists are finding that a lot happens very quickly if an individual's levels of emotional and physiological arousal remain elevated and unchecked. The intervention of choice for mitigating this is PFA—an evidence-informed modular approach for assisting people in the immediate aftermath of disasters, terrorism and other violent events. The goal is to reduce initial distress, and to foster short- and long-term adaptive functioning.

If you are in a lockdown and subject to an emergency response from an external group, such as an Employee Assistance Program (EAP) provider for psychological support, it may be several hours before you are able to leave the building or days before such services are made available. Neuroscience indicates that a delay in providing psychological support to address the emotional impact of the incident can result in lasting psychological repercussions. The best tactical option is developing an internal psychological first aid response capability. Relying on your company's EAP will not always suffice because they most likely will not be entering the hot zone—they simply will not have access to the scene in a timely manner. Whoever is part of that locked-down group can and should be the first initial providers of psychological support.

The PFA skill set can be introduced to a limited number of employees— analogous to the employee fire marshals that most companies have on each floor of their office building or the ranks of employees trained in CPR or use of AED equipment. PFA skills are not reserved for medical or mental health professionals. Anybody can be trained in this model of "buddy supports." As with a fire marshal, two or three people per floor is optimal, providing some redundancy in case an incident occurs on the day that one or more of the trained colleagues are out of the office.

Evaluate your work environment and consider how it is structured. Whether it is an office, a factory or a retail environment, you need to consider how best to use the PFA model to ensure that there will always be at least one or two trained employees available. This can be perhaps five percent of the workforce—one out of every 20. Ideally, you should have as many people in the workforce trained in psychological first aid as you do for something like CPR.

The nationally recognized model of PFA was developed jointly with the National Children's Traumatic Stress Network (NCTSN) in cooperation with the National Center for Posttraumatic Stress Disorder (NCPTSD). The Psychological First Aid Field Operations Guide 2nd edition, is available at the NCPTSD website (http://www.ncptsd.va.gov), and fully explains what is now considered to be the intervention of choice by the National Academy of Sciences in the immediate aftermath of traumatic events. As a subject-matter expert, I participated in some of the federal government teams that refined this approach to intervention, so I am very familiar with psychological first aid strategies and techniques. I've also conducted countless training sessions for organizations of all types and sizes, where I have seen PFA successfully implemented and put to good use in the aftermath of actual crisis events.

PFA is a very useful tool for managing the emotional impact of violent events, but unfortunately many organizations don't find out about it until after the fact. Developing the capacity to provide PFA in the immediate wake of a crisis is something you should not overlook in your efforts to develop a comprehensive workplace violence prevention program.

Preparing for Unconventional Violence

Workplace violence can take many forms, and as we all know, the world is getting more unpredictable every day. It's therefore ever more important to think outside the box when designing your awareness program.

What would you do if someday you received a white powdered letter in the mail? I even heard of a case where an employee put mercury on the upholstery of a coworker's chair and poisoned her. This stuff is real, so you need to start talking now about unconventional violence in the workplace beyond the shooter.

We tend to think about the white powered letter as being terrorism, but as I point out in Chapter 1, terrorism and "true believers" are a major category of perpetrators that need to be given equal weight with any other. These unconventional acts of violence can be perpetrated by employees, former employees, domestic partners and any disturbed person who walks onto the premises.

The behavioral element in this discussion is where organizations can easily get it wrong. If the assumptions that inform your workplace violence posture assume specific, somewhat conventional factors in prediction, response and recovery, and then an unanticipated event occurs—say, a bioterrorism scenario—you may find that your response and recovery are dramatically different.

You may get a radically different outcome in terms of people's behavior than if your workplace violence plan is based only around an active shooter situation, and then an employee in the mail room or the accounting department opens an envelope only to have white powder spill in her lap. This can be as terrifying, or more terrifying, than when shots are fired.

"There are significant behavioral differences between conventional and unconventional terrorism." notes Steven Crimando. "If you are going to have the discussion about terrorism, for example, along behavioral lines, then conventional terrorism is bombing, shooting and kidnapping, whereas unconventional terrorism is the WMD sorts of scenarios, potentially involving biological and radiological materials. The responses to each of these can radically differ from one another, and that must be taken into account."

The Ethical Component

Finally, when all is said and done, there is the ethical aspect of making workplace violence prevention everyone's job. You may have seen ABC's popular hidden camera show, called "What Would You Do?," in which unsuspecting members of the public are presented with ethically challenging dilemmas that touch on bullying and abuse, lying, racism, parenting and more. It makes for interesting viewing, and drives home the fact that people can sometimes lose their ethical bearings when presented with challenging situations where, "doing the right thing" may not be the easiest course of action.

Ethical decision making is at the center of that show's concept, and also is a big part of this idea of everyone taking responsibility for an organization's safety. After all, people are faced with ethical decisions all the time. It's not unlike the situations on that show, or when you observe someone hitting back five or six shots of Tequila in a bar. In that case, how often does anyone then step up to say "you can't drive your car"? The workplace analogy to this is when people start to observe irrational, inappropriate or bizarre behavior in their work environment. Our question is, at what point will coworkers or supervisors step up and say we've got to interact with that; something has to be done.

So ask yourself: To what extent has your organization fostered this ethos? What programs have you put in place to do so, and what has been your experience?

Everyone taking an active role in workplace violence prevention is doing good practice for safety, morale and business success. It's also a good deed, the right thing to do, for those who may be moving toward violence as a solution to their problems, the possible victim or victims of that violence and for anyone unintentionally caught in the line of fire. If you point this out to your employees—if you stand up and say "We have a potential situation here, and we need to take action"—you will be setting an example that will support your entire workplace violence prevention program and encourage others to do the same. That's the type of thing that should be rewarded, recognized and encouraged.

GUEST EXPERT
Leadership's Role in Making Prevention Everyone's Job

By Ron Rabena, *Division President, AlliedBarton Security Services*

As organizational leaders we have an obligation to make sure that every employee takes ownership of safety in the workplace. Being a better leader means examining the situation, talking in depth with the people involved, and passing that information through the appropriate channels to correct any issue. That attitude and practice must permeate the organization.

To make sure this happens, leaders need to give employees the right tools, clearly communicating to them the workplace violence prevention message and their expectations. You must support their obligation to get involved to correct a developing situation, getting ahead of the issue by employing direct attention and use of any assistance programs that may be available. Training, followed by confirmation that employees understand what is expected of them, is critical, because if you have people who are not engaged, it's not going to work. The more focus you put on his topic, the more you can raise awareness; the more examples you can give people, the better off you're going to be.

Effective workplace violence education and response can, of course, be hindered by misconceptions about what workplace violence actually is, and where it is likely to occur. Take, for example, the myth that "it can't happen here." In 2010 a horrible workplace violence incident was reported at a food processing plant in Philadelphia. According to news accounts, a woman who had been suspended from her job there returned with a handgun and opened fire, killing two people and critically injuring a third before being taken into custody. Accounts of the incident noted that this was a situation where everyone there knew of this woman's unsettling behavior and used to joke that someday she was going to "go postal."

A few years ago there was another situation in the news—that of a lone gunman, described as a disgruntled investor, who entered the Philadelphia Naval Business Center and killed three people at a board meeting before turning the gun on himself.

The takeaway is that nobody is immune to this. These incidents drive home the fact that workplace violence can happen anywhere, and preventing it comes down to building that all-important awareness as fostered through ongoing education and training programs within the organization. Open-door policies and hotlines managed by HR are important to help give every employee the organizational support he or she needs to feel comfortable with reporting the unusual or ominous behavior of a colleague.

You have to knock down those walls of hesitation and fear, making a new atmosphere of engagement part of an organization's culture. It all begins with hiring—when a prospective employee walks in the door—and continues with orientation, training and beyond, reinforcing this attitude during the work experience and doing temperature checks along the way.

This is more than just a smart way to run an organization. It goes beyond prudent HR practices, and beyond what might be an employer's "legal responsibilities." When it comes to possibly preventing a horrific act of workplace violence, we all have a responsibility as human beings, which is if you see something, say something. When you observe something that's out of the ordinary, report what you see to the proper authorities, whether to security, HR or over a hotline.

We have an obligation to ourselves, to the people around us, to the organization for which we work, and to any innocent bystanders who could get hurt if something happens. At AlliedBarton our personal and business values are aligned. We respect people, and at the same time we have an obligation to respond appropriately when called upon. At the end of the day, it's the right thing to do.

Part Three

Applying Next Practices
for Success

chapter 9

Strategies for a Secure High-Performance Organization

ctually putting a comprehensive workplace violence prevention
program into place is where the proverbial rubber meets the road
—where you put together all of the understandings, strategies and
practices I've described in this book. Such a program should incorporate a
realistic understanding of the truths and myths about workplace violence
prevention, coupled with next practices for leadership, employee engagement and professional growth for everyone in your organization.

Throughout this book I've used AlliedBarton's own philosophies, programs, policies and culture as examples for how you can build a stronger and
safer workplace. I'm proud of what we've accomplished, and believe that a lot
of what we've done can serve as good models for your own efforts. That's not
to say that we're perfect—we still have plenty of work to do. Securing my
organization is an ongoing work in progress, as it would be anywhere. It's a
living, evolving process.

In Chapter 2 I discuss at length how easy it is for people and organizations
to fall into a culture of falsehoods about violence at work, and to slip into the
belief that "Because it has not happened here, it will not happen here." The whole
topic of workplace violence tends to scare people, and that fear translates easily
into avoidance and inaction. As I've repeated multiple times in these pages, inaction is risky, and ultimately can be costly to your organization.

The foundation of your prevention strategy means building a culture
of awareness and leadership, enabling your employees to take action if
needed—all practices that I cover at length in Part Two of this book. The
more you enable people to address and respond to milder levels of violence,

such as threats, bullying or inappropriate verbal intimidation, the more likely it is you can head off more aggressive higher-order violence in your organizational culture.

Next-practice thinking and models are important tools for building and executing a superior workplace violence prevention program that will meet or exceed an organization's legal and ethical obligations. As I discuss in Chapter 4, conventional best practices can be enhanced further with next-practice thinking to more effectively address variable situations, as well as uncertain future incidents or contingencies.

Next practice–style models and frameworks, like the workplace violence continuum, can show complex relationships in a very accessible way. The continuum is designed to help you see different types of workplace violence behaviors in context. This will help you recognize specific behaviors in your workplace and put them into a meaningful context so you can respond appropriately. Other next-practice tools might include decision matrices, risk assessment tools, and behavioral assessment models used to evaluate individual activities.

In this chapter I offer an overview of workplace violence prevention policymaking, along with some additional thoughts and guidance for implementing your own program.

Building Relationships

I think the best key for understanding this whole strategic universe of workplace violence as it relates to your security and performance is relationships. Certainly, you need the grounding of fact-based research about workplace violence as the underpinning of any program, but your in-house effort is really about building, maintaining and growing relationships between your employees, managers and executives, and continually educating them through dialog on the need to be aware of the risks and dangers of violence. The quality and power of that dialog has, I believe, the opportunity to be the basis for enhanced business performance, simply because it will bring about new levels of trust and openness to your organization.

Building a workplace violence prevention strategy comes from the top. Executing it has to be a company-wide effort. If people don't have skin in the game, it simply won't be effective. People must take responsibility for their own security and get involved at every level.

Ultimately, building this strategy is about putting all the pieces together to make a functional, workable program that helps your company defeat workplace violence and also grow as an organization in the process. By facing up to the challenge, you become a bigger, better and more effective organization. That's a win for everybody.

Creating a Prevention Policy

How do you take effective steps to offset falsehoods and the incorrect perceptions that many people have and build a proactive culture to deal with violence? One of the most basic ways an organization can build a foundation for action is a written policy that establishes and communicates to its employees—one that establishes its fundamental definitions, rules, security policies and other details. A company policy is one of the most basic tools to prevent workplace violence simply because it raises visibility and makes all employees aware.

Organizations have numerous reasons to create a workplace violence policy. From the vantage point of pure political and business calculation, it's a good way to guard against exposure from future risks and liabilities if something bad did happen—a tangible way of showing how your company takes action. Then, there's the business calculation: It's an investment in the overall safety and security of the company, its reputation and its brand image. And of course, there's a reason to do it for the collective good of the safety of the employees and the whole human culture in the company, which is the most compelling reason of all.

The policy serves to both define workplace violence as the company views its potential impact upon the organization, as well as to identify the appropriate levels of response to key incidents and types of violent actions. Such a policy can be communicated to employees to clearly define the range of acceptable and nonacceptable behaviors. Some companies may limit their definition of workplace violence to extreme incidents of physical assault, while others may include threats and physical intimidation as violent events. Still others may recognize verbal abuse and bullying in the category of workplace violence, which is what I strongly recommend.

Higher-order violent behaviors such as assault or use of a weapon are obvious and are typically cited in any workplace violence policy. What is more subtle and less recognized is the level of milder or intermediate threat

Workplace Violence Continuum

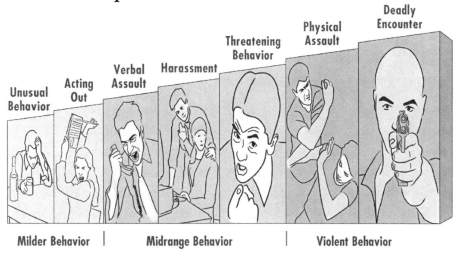

Workplace violence is an active continuum of behaviors.

levels that the company choses to distinguish and classify in its policy as violent behavior.

We designed the continuum specifically to help readers of this book understand the relationships of key violent behaviors. What is significant from both a policy and business-performance standpoint is that milder and midrange violent behaviors are likely to be more frequent than higher order violent behaviors. The question becomes this: At what point does relatively common social behavior in a business context, perhaps a manager or coworker vigorously correcting or expressing displeasure with a subordinate, progress from acceptable business conduct into abusive, violent behavior?

Defining that fine line is not easy. It is perhaps why some companies shy away from the challenge and find it easier to box off the workplace violence issue as an easily identified, narrowly defined, extreme behavior that might never happen. That's all well and good, and that may brush some uncomfortable issues under the rug, but in my view it fundamentally misses the point.

A workplace violence prevention policy gives you an opportunity to confront some real demons in your business culture, and to empower your employees to handle them collectively. By facing up to the fine line between acceptable, aggressive and direct business behavior and abusiveness, you can use the policy to create a collaborative culture that has many second-order benefits, including the following:

- ✤ Directly addressing abusive interactions in your business culture
- ✤ Supporting and developing a collaborative culture of problem resolution
- ✤ Motivating employees with your concern for their safety and well-being at work
- ✤ Creating an ongoing environment for improving performance
- ✤ Building an internally secure culture based upon mutual respect

Zero Tolerance

"Zero tolerance" is a concept that I tend to revisit again and again, and such policies have gained ground as a safe and secure strategy in recent years. To me, it reflects and supports advance education and awareness, as well as a demonstration by every organizational colleague that they understand and live by the values of workplace violence prevention. This concept aligns with the next-practices thinking that I feel is critical. By embracing appropriate behavior, and by anticipating any future situation, and then modeling those factors for employees, you can head off unwanted situations before they take place. This is far superior to putting your organization in situations where you have to wait around like sitting ducks with policies that are designed to react only to certain scenarios.

Many base their zero-tolerance policies on absolute definitions of unacceptable behaviors, and prescribe strict to absolute responses. This approach can be useful in setting a cultural standard, but given the often-variable context and perceptions around incidents involving mild or midrange behaviors profiled in our continuum, it also can be problematic at times, putting the organization and its managers into strict either-or decisions of firing an employee after an identified incident, or excepting or ignoring the policy, thus undercutting its effectiveness.

Therefore, I strongly recommend "zero tolerance" as a standard for organizational behavior, but obviously, there always are gray areas that may need to be taken into account on a case-by-case basis depending on the specific situation.

Visioning Your Policy

Participation of all parties in developing your workplace violence prevention policy is an absolute requirement to its success. It's amazing to me how some executives or even managers will get proprietary about something like this, assume temporary or permanent ownership of it, and then turn up with a document draft they try to force down everybody else's throats. This will not work. A workplace violence policy is a company-wide effort, and the more broadly the ownership and authorship is shared, the better. C-suite executives, managers, supervisors, HR and the security staff should all be involved. Each department should appoint a champion to participate with the team in writing the policy and then report back to their group. Keep it open, transparent and participatory.

Once in place, training, promotion, testing and periodic "check-ins" are essential. A workplace violence policy must be a living document. People must be reminded of the contents and what is going on, what is new affecting the policy and what their responsibilities are. And yes, people must be updated with reports when incidents occur. The overall goal here is to raise awareness and make people connected to the organizational culture.

In the final analysis, workplace violence policies transform knowledge into structure and action for organizations. They give employees a fundamental performance standard. The telling issue is whether the organization does the absolute minimum, in which case they are missing an opportunity to use this as a springboard to build a much more rewarding and collaborative culture than existed before.

Implementing Internal Control Programs

Research shows that a comprehensive workplace violence prevention program is the most effective way to reduce risk. Work done by acclaimed organizational theorist and author Chris Argyris helps make the case for this. Argyris documented how formal organizations, control systems and management structures interact with individuals and how they responded and adapted to them. His work has become the basis of effective control programs that enable a functional management structure to achieve a common goal.

For a workplace violence control program, you focus upon a core initiative built around employee education and awareness in combination with the following factors:

 ⁕ An ongoing, visible demonstration of your and your managers' personal commitment to guarding against workplace violence.

→ Control components and tools used consistently, such as communications, monthly updates and the workplace violence continuum.

→ Regular reviews and testing of employee awareness, the effectiveness of controls and their impact on finance, operations, compliance and risk management.

Boiling it down, the core concept of a control program is "bringing it all together." Workplace violence is a complex dynamic made up of many multiple levels of behaviors combined with different types of perpetrators, motivations, triggers and context issues. Our responses to it are equally as complex. We have to focus our collective understanding of the situation, our tools and our resources in order to create a foundation for dialog and support throughout the organization, from the executives through every department all the way to the shipping docks or the shop floor.

The control program becomes the spine, the central element we can use to hang all these elements upon and make them work together as a single entity. This can include the organization's written policy and any specific methods we use in support of that policy and the specific behaviors, responses and tools it entails.

It's important to emphasize that each organization has a different level of exposure to workplace violence, and therefore individual control programs will differ. Retail establishments, particularly smaller fast-food locations and 24x7 convenience stores, are more frequently targeted for criminal activity, so they must develop defensive plans specific to their risk in ways that may differ from those of a manufacturing company working out of a factory site. Each control program must be an intelligent aggregation of tools that respond to the specific level and depth of risk facing that particular business.

Control programs are an integrated solution that can be continually tested and evaluated for effectiveness against your overall prevention strategy. Having a structure in place is key because it gives you a solid base benchmark from which to continually reevaluate your program's effectiveness. Organizations that have random responses to workplace violence, or poorly integrated responses to violent behaviors such as sexual harassment, often can miss the challenge and do not address real issues. With responses scattered over hit-and-miss programs, their effectiveness is diluted and lacking in structure, providing little focus or ability to effectively review and improve the environment going forwarded.

These programs work best when implemented through cross-functional teams, which is a classic next-practices approach. The more you can bring to the table different points of view for updating the system, the more effectively and rapidly you can manage and build effective control programs for workplace violence. Using a standard security team is good, but using a broader cross-functional group is better, simply because the wider dialog will give you more perspectives and ultimately, more buy-in.

Working together and cross-sharing information is critical for the success of internal control programs. Different departments know different details. What the HR department knows about human behavior in the organization can be valuable in context with what the security department knows about physical security on the worksite. Little things are significant. Departing employees often tell you more about bullying, poor behavior and other incidents in an exit interview to HR than will active employees. So, we have to make an effort to capture that, building and sharing the knowledge.

The Airborne Express Comprehensive Prevention Model

Airborne Express has made violence prevention a corporate priority. Rather than using just a few specific security measures, the organization attributes its success to a seven-pronged approach. Here is a summary of the main points provided in an address on workplace violence to a congressional subcommittee:

1. A strict zero-tolerance policy with regard to any act or threat of violence made by an employee. Violations make the employee immediately subject to discipline, up to and including termination, regardless of that employee's position or seniority within the company.

2. Background screening featuring a seven-year criminal background check; a 10-year previous employment check; a 10-year previous residency check; a five-year credit history check; and a three-year motor vehicle records check.

3. Drug testing at the time of hire and random drug and alcohol testing for those in safety-sensitive positions.

4. Physical security measures to enhance personal security, including security officers, restricted entrances, bright lighting, key cards, alarms and various types of surveillance systems.

5. A strict no-weapons policy.

6. A consistent termination policy.

7. A crisis-management program specifically designed to respond to any incident or threat of violence made by or against an employee.

Source: IOFM Report

Realistic Security Procedures

Security is a core aspect of a workplace violence program. There is, of course, physical security, guarding a physical space with security officers and hard perimeters. Other forms of security rely on intelligent, advance planning— modeling potential threats and situations so that you can frame your response and be ready in advance. Employee education and involvement is central to an effective security plan, as I have addressed with specific focus points and actionable suggestions in Chapter 8.

Professional security staff is another key component. Their perspectives should be brought together with leadership to engage the larger organization in examining the security procedures that should be in place supporting workplace violence.

A security procedures assessment helps focus on policies and processes that could reduce future risks. It can be very wide-ranging, encompassing human capital practices, physical security processes and guidelines for interaction with the public. This assessment should include a thorough survey and assessment of community crime rates, physical security attributes of the site, unique industry risks, the potential of violent behavior within employee and visitor populations and the attractiveness of the facility as a target. This type of assessment can provide distinctively different or even alternative points of view on the security challenges facing you, which then can be considered in drafting a balanced, effective plan.

One particular challenge that workplace violence represents for security is defining the line between acceptable and unacceptable behavior at the lower ends of the continuum. When you have a bullying or a confrontational event involving two employees, what are the identifying behaviors that clearly establish it as unacceptable behavior? To some extent situations like these may require reporting and some level of corroborating evidence and value judgment based on evidence or claims. The security question here will turn on how to absolutely define and identify that unacceptable behavior so it can be reported and you can then take some form of corrective action.

In the workplace violence universe, security will take the form of communication as much as it takes the form of physical perimeters in other contexts in the company. The security function will focus on communicating and modeling standards and expectations of behavior to make sure all employees understand the boundaries. Security-as-prevention will mean a very strong emphasis upon anticipating and drilling on responses to workplace violence scenarios. The focal point will be the overall improvement of the company life and the improvement to employee safety.

ROUNDTABLE
Selling Workplace Violence Prevention to Leadership

Bill Whitmore, *Chairman & CEO, AlliedBarton Security Services*
Bonnie Michelman, *Director of Police and Outside Services, Massachusetts General Hospital*
Maureen Rush, *Vice President for Public Safety, University of Pennsylvania*
Chris Swecker, *former Assistant Director Criminal Investigative Division,* FBI
Patrick J. Wolfe, *former Vice President for Corporate Security, Cigna Corporation, retired U.S. Secret Service*

Bill Whitmore: If you go to a decision maker at your organization and you want to make the case for a greater emphasis on workplace violence prevention with a more formalized effort or program, what do you say? We heard the reputational argument, we heard about the negligence lawsuits. What other sorts of arguments can you make—how it affects productivity?

Chris Swecker: We couldn't do it without some higher-level executive sponsorship. Management doesn't like to scare people, and to them it's sort of like that dirty little secret that you don't want to pull out of the closet too often in these hyper-sensitive corporations. So the biggest challenge really is getting the sponsorship to drive this whole awareness issue deep into the organization. Recognition is needed at the supervisory level so that employees feel that they have some mandate to act.

Patrick J. Wolfe: I would recommend what I did at one point: an active report delivered personally every month to my manager. The chairman received the report summary twice a year. In these kinds of reports, the facts speak for themselves. For example, "Harriet was approached by her husband James at work, who then hit her." More than anything else, this report helped engage our leadership. These are smart people, so you can present the value proposition that if an incident occurs with the company it is going to affect the branding. And they are going to lose production for maybe three or five days. And they are going to have issues at that site for a long time.

Bonnie Michelman: I recently started doing a report to the executive management team every month laying out all the incidents. I wanted it to be a realistic view of workplace violence. They see the fact that on any given week we can have a couple of dozen people being severely threatened, and that's what I need.

Whitmore: In some organizations the problem might be that report might not be happening or going up high enough into leadership, or perhaps it is sequestered in HR.

Swecker: A former boss questioned me about what was going on, so I did a report about all the incidents just to create some awareness. But then the dissemination group got wider and wider, getting close to 100 people. At one point we actually sat down with the top five executives and asked them "do you want to see this?" And all five said yes. But then as more bad news kept coming out, my boss asked "are you sure you want to circulate this?"

Whitmore: It would be interesting to know how many corporations actually evaluate the cost of lost productivity and turnover caused by workplace violence. Bank of America, the University of Pennsylvania, Mass General—because of their profile being open to the public all day— may get this more than other organizations. Is it embedded in the culture? If you had a scorecard and you said 90 percent of our beds were filled last night, we saw everyone in the ER within 14 minutes. If there were KPIs around workplace violence, would it help?

Wolfe: Training is very important but it is also a cost but one that is extremely difficult to quantify. We can quantify our concerns by cross checking our incident reports. If we have reports of an unusual amount threats coming from one site, we can go to the local human resources staff and compare our reports to theirs.

Maureen Rush: And it's a point that everyone in this room who has been in some level of law enforcement or security knows—if you don't document it, it didn't happen, and therefore you can't qualify it as ROI. They are going to need to put workplace violence information in the training package in order to count it as a ROI.

Whitmore: When you talk to people about this, the conversation has to absolutely include the financials. If I accept that this is a festering problem, I might have to spend a significant sum of money during the year to address it, and that's going to affect my next three quarters. Or, am I going to ignore it now, and when something happens I have to spend exponentially more to fix it?

Rush: They also think that it's true to a degree that no matter how much security you put into something, there's a lawyer that's going to take the case and you are going to get sued. Now on the civil side, with a robust prevention program you can at least defend the situation by saying you did everything possible to prevent this. From a money point of view, they are probably saying if I spend $10 million every year and if nothing happens for 15 years, well I'll just take that hit in the 15th year and hire a bunch of PR people to smooth over our reputation. So I think that often it is about money, and I think the second thing is awareness. When we don't inform our people, or they just refuse to be informed, then we have problems in our environments. If they can't feel that, if we can't get that in their gut, they are never going to believe what comes out of our mouths.

Michelman: It's hard to quantify what we deter or what we prevent. This is the difficulty of our profession and a proactive program.

Wolfe: We can show by our daily reports. Let's say we have a lot of threats coming from the call center, we can go to HR and say what's going on? Usually there is a production problem and/or a morale issue at that site.

Whitmore: Three things: high turnover, high overtime, high HR complaints.

Michelman: You just raised turnover and I think that is a really important point. You need to get across to people that every time you prevent a person from leaving a job, you are saving about $60,000 on average for a midrange person in this country today…that's a lot of money. This includes productivity loss, rehiring, training and so forth. Many people leave a job if they don't feel safe, and that can cost you.

Employee Screening

Background screening is a good tactic to help filter prospective employees from a workplace violence standpoint. This method is thought by many experts to help minimize employee-on-employee violence in its most extreme and violent form.

The minimum screen is a careful check of criminal history records. Other layers of detail include verification of work history, places of employment and length of time on the job, educational background verification, personal and professional references, verification of licenses, motor vehicle checks, credit records, drug screening and personality testing. Based on 1.7 million individual background checks completed by Automatic Data Processing (ADP) in the 2008 calendar year, six percent revealed a criminal record in the past seven years, according to the Institute of Financial Management (IOFM). In select industries, nearly one in 10 applicants has a recent criminal record.

Routine use of background checks can help increase the safety of the workplace significantly. In the same way drug screening can help minimize substance abuse, screening for workplace violence markers such as criminal background or history of violent incidents in the past can help to minimize the number of new hires that come into the organization with a predisposition to violence or disruptive behavior. Background and reference checks are a key element in getting a clear sense of the propensities of an employment candidate. Companies must have a strong sense of will and commitment as well—to communicate company values in the prehire stage to candidates that it is a serious issue at this company.

Gaps in the System

Internet-based searches and systems have made background checking easier to perform, and most security and HR professionals commonly conduct them. However, there are gaps in the system. Job applicants coming into the company are likely to get the full screening treatment, whereas current employees on a promotion path to new responsibilities may not be screened in line with their new responsibilities. Vendors and the extended network of resources such as consultants are rarely screened and can represent an unknown quantity. We are interdependent on each other to deploy acceptable, comprehensive record checks.

Another questionable area is social networking. Studies show that 51 percent of people use social networking sites to screen people, but these are usually a hodgepodge of content placed by the individual page holder, friends and associates. There is little in social networks that can be absolutely identified as fact, because most of the content there is random and often posted on a whim, subject to slight knowledge of activities, bursts of emotion and even grudges. You really have to take what you read there with a large grain of salt. The one potential benefit that social network sites do offer is that they often contain photographs of the individual in various contexts, providing an identity verification resource.

Nationwide Background Screening

This country has no real national screening database that any organization can access, and that's a real issue for me—one that I harp on again and again when I speak at conferences. Not having a national database that we all can access puts many of us at a real disadvantage as far as security is concerned. Because laws and standards can vary from state to state, high-risk individuals can slip through the cracks.

Hopefully we can get a legitimate and useful database of this kind established in the very near future. I discuss the need for an accessible national screening database further in Chapter 11.

Use Your Judgment

Screening employees for workplace violence is an inexact art, to put it candidly. Some states restrict how you can use criminal backgrounds in screening a perspective employee, and screening of any sort has to be used as a filter. We can't necessarily draw a straight line between any data point and say this person is a threat for sure and that person isn't. We can suggest that where allowed you screen for people that you likely don't want to have in your organization in any case—people with criminal background histories, particularly people with any kind of history of violent action or events in their past. It's not enough to just gather that information, you have to use it in the hiring process to correlate and connect so you really get a whole picture of the person. Make sure everything lines up and all the dots line up and the lines connect correctly. The best goal here is to catch problem cases before they get entrenched in your organization and become a festering point for problems that you have to manage in the future.

Beyond the Behavioral: Securing Facilities

Many buildings can be vulnerable to violent attack. People come and go despite the most stringent security measures. That tightened up somewhat after 9/11. The greatest risks and vulnerabilities are by a known person, such as the disgruntled individual who may have a beef with the company or any of its employees.

Access to buildings is much more than just doors, locks and bolts. It is the systems behind the physical apparatus, and the determination behind the systems. The essentials of physical security are important but can be disarmingly obvious to the point of commonplace. Better locks, better lighting, alarms, security cameras—those are the superficial things. The deeper things about securing access to a building are the essentials of attention. Are the security officers paying attention? What are they watching for? How are they using the basic physical tools of security to monitor access to the building?

Securing a company's buildings and worksites on a day-to-day basis from violence is a critical factor in the battle against workplace violence. It's not a situation where you are likely to have a shooter trying to get in every day, but there are unknown levels of risk operating all the time. A company should be constantly preparing and refining a security operation that monitors access to its sites to protect the safety of its employees and its customers. Maybe there will be a threat that takes place one day in ten years. The purpose of your work is to be ready to manage that threat successfully on that one day so there are no catastrophic consequences.

Beyond the deeper and more sophisticated strategies for physical security, which are outside the scope of this book, the real focus of securing your facilities is observation: structuring your security team to see correctly as people come into the building and be aware, to question and to monitor. All the physical security tools and systems in the world are there to support intelligent human insight that is watching and asking the right questions that will truly make you safe.

When Violence Happens

Since 2008 there has been a rise in workplace violence that many experts believe is closely associated with the increasing pressure people are feeling at work and overall uncertainty about jobs nationally. Stress or conflict at work, financial issues and even trouble at home can all contribute to workplace violence.

Employers are becoming more aware of the need to have policies and procedures in place that will guide employees who may come face-to-face with someone intent on doing harm.

For those who find themselves in a violent situation, whether physical or verbal, there are some things they should try to remember. As part of your overall workplace violence prevention effort, employees should be drilled and tested periodically so that they will be better prepared to act in a worst-case scenario.

When violence breaks out in the workplace, you are faced with three options: run, hide or take action.

If you do find yourself in a close encounter with someone intent on inflicting harm, you or those you work with will probably not be able to run or hide. "Take action" includes many scenarios, but if having to talk to a person bent on violence is the situation you've found yourself in, this advice may be helpful:

* **Remain calm:** The calmer you are, the better you will be able to think about how to properly handle the situation. You may also make others feel safer if you are calm and not panicked.

* **Stance and body language:** The way you present yourself is critical. It is your goal to help defuse the attacker's anger and get the person to remain calm. The attacker has to believe you are not going to attack them, and the way you stand can reinforce that. Use a slightly open stance with one foot behind the other and most of your weight on your back foot. Not only does this convey a neutral signal but it also gives you more freedom to react should you be attacked.

* **Do not raise your voice:** Speak in a normal, even tone.

* **Listen, listen and listen:** Maybe the attacker just wants to be heard. Let them vent and do not interrupt or argue with him or her.

✦ **Think before you speak:** Certain comments could confuse the attacker or imply that your opinions are more important than theirs. Ask the attacker, "I can see that you are upset. How can I help?" Avoid using these phrases:

  – "I know how you feel."

  – "You shouldn't be angry. It is no big deal."

  – "Don't worry about it. You'll be fine."

✦ **Don't take anything personally:** People who have reached the point where they are prepared to act out violently might be looking for someone to take their side and get emotionally involved in their issue.

✦ **Be mindful of your facial expressions:** You can nod to indicate that you understand what is being said, but you should be careful about openly agreeing or disagreeing. The idea, again, is to let the person talk.

✦ **Keep your hands in view of the attacker:** Your palms might be sweaty from nerves but it is better to show your palms to the attacker rather than crossing your arms or making a fist. This conveys a nonconfrontational demeanor and also shows the attacker that you are not armed.

✦ **Eye contact:** Maintain regular eye contact with the attacker but don't stare at or try to stare him down. The idea is to use eye contact to "connect" and build a level of trust that might help the attacker continue talking and calm down.

✦ **If a weapon is involved:** Follow the attacker's orders. Unless you are certain that your life is in immediate danger, you should not try to disarm an attacker.

✦ **Getting help:** In all violent situations, be sure to call 911 as soon as possible. Fully cooperate with arriving police and keep your hands visible to them, as they have no way of knowing who the attacker is and who may be an innocent bystander.

The most important way you can contribute to the successful outcome of a violent confrontation in the workplace is to be informed and alert, remain calm and contact a manager or police as soon as you witness violent or potentially violent behavior in the workplace. Workplace violence can happen in any environment, any industry, so it is important to understand how to handle a violent workplace situation.

Selling Workplace Violence Prevention to Senior Management

Regardless of your level in the organization—from CEO to regional manager, division manager or department head—creating a comprehensive program using the principles in this book is going to require buy-in from your colleagues to get it launched and funded. A lot of well-intentioned executives see that as a challenging prospect, because you're proposing to dedicate resources to a problem that may not be particularly visible or intuitive. You're proposing additional costs in an area where ROI is not nearly as obvious as when you're acquiring a company, investing in a cutting-edge technology or marketing a new product.

I think people like to project an "aura of wisdom" on the c-suite of their company. Maybe it's just wishful thinking, but employees certainly hope their leadership is all-seeing, all-knowing and fully up to the challenges of successfully navigating the company through all the rocks and storms. In practice, I have found c-suite leaders are subject to many of the same errors of perception and challenges as most people. It's just as easy for a major corporate CEO or CFO to buy into myths about workplace violence as it is for a line manager in the factory. Workplace violence scares everybody. It's an equal opportunity threat to our emotional equilibrium, and therefore it's much easier to pretend it is simply not there.

The challenge I have found with getting workplace violence prevention the attention it needs in the c-suite comes down to one word: bandwidth. Leadership of big companies have so much on their plate to keep a business running that a lot of critical issues get short shrift and scant attention. This makes it necessary to raise the level of urgency, making the issue of violence at work visceral and real for the leadership—first by countering falsehoods, and then portraying the reality—perhaps through a monthly report that raises awareness among the top decision makers.

Bringing the issue home makes people uncomfortable but it also creates the basis for urgent action. Monthly reports can create a consistent reality base that helps break the grip of falsehoods. It helps executives come clean to the clear and present reality of day-to-day violence in our world, and to the clear and present danger it could represent to their employees first and their brand second.

The big risk at high levels is that you get some kind of recognition followed by a Band-Aid solution. In the case of workplace violence prevention, that usually takes the form of a pro-forma company policy—underfunded, tepidly supported and casually enforced and communicated. For some organizations, workplace violence remains a touchy topic that they would rather sweep under the rug than openly discuss.

Proving Return on Investment

Workplace violence is estimated to cost $12 billion a year to American corporations. This is a staggering number. Maybe that's because studies have shown that it is 100 times more costly to react to an incident versus preventing one.

At the highest level there is a fundamental argument that the company is better off by managing its exposure to workplace violence. First, by ensuring the safety of its employees, and second, by taking steps to minimize any negative impact on its brand that an episode would entail.

There's an even bigger jump in contending that by investing in a collaborative, high-communication culture of zero tolerance of workplace violence—threats, intimidation and so forth—the company can build a much more effective high-performance culture. It's always hard to really grind the numbers and prove an ROI case perfectly and this one is no easier than any of the others. But I believe it is there fundamentally.

Employees who understand that the organization is investing in their welfare, taking care of their safety at work, are going to be more motivated than those occupying a workplace that is disrupted by violent episodes where they do not feel personally secure. There's also the fact that violent incidents on any level will cause poor morale, leading to higher turnover, which can create huge annual retraining costs for any organization.

Engaging executives around workplace violence has to start somewhere. Often the most commonplace point of organization and reference is a workplace violence policy.

This is potentially where the secure, high-performance effort can take off.

Securing the High-Performance Organization

Securing your workplace against workplace violence should be a fundamental goal of your organization, with each of the fundamental moving parts profiled in this chapter acting as elements in the overall strategy. Fundamentally, these practices all entail a recognition of core cultural values that help to secure the organization from risk.

The whole idea of workplace violence should engender a positive core value of safety. Your entire employee base can work toward that goal both as a means of securing people and the overall organization, and as a performance target. People who feel they are in a safe and secure environment are capable of achieving great things. It is up to their leaders to tap into this fundamental optimism and allegiance, and move them forward to success.

GUEST EXPERT
Effective Crisis Planning for College Campuses

By Glenn R. Rosenberg, *Vice President, Higher Education, AlliedBarton Security Services*

It's no surprise that shooting incidents and other tragedies on college campuses generate national headlines. Fortunately, active shooters on campus are extraordinarily rare events, and university environments remain far safer than the community at large. Nevertheless, colleges and universities that experience adversity will need to be able to manage it effectively.

An incident response plan provides a framework within which a college or university can manage the crisis, creating clear and defined objectives for the institution's recovery. These plans include operational and strategic overviews to ensure that a crisis is contained and controlled properly. Management skills in communicating with staff, students, the media and the community, together with the ability of management to determine post-crisis goals and recovery strategies, can determine the college's survival prospects.

Creating a truly effective plan requires the partnership of campus administration, municipal law enforcement and emergency services, and campus police and security. The federal government has mandated and encouraged the use of the National Incident Management System's (NIMS) Incident Command System (ICS) to ensure interoperability and cooperation of all responding parties. Ultimately, effective planning requires collaboration, foresight, diligence and a plan that is actively tested with mock disaster scenarios. While each recovery plan must be developed to an institution's unique needs, including student population, geographic locations, and other variables, there are numerous common elements that have been defined in work done jointly by the Department of Homeland Security and the International Association of Campus Law Enforcement Administrators (IACLEA). These planning templates help an institution think through the varied aspects of the planned response.

A very specific and specialized Critical Incident Management System class was created by BowMac Educational Services, Inc., licensed to IACLEA and funded by Homeland Security. This unique "simulation-based" training course features use of the "7 Critical Tasks®" in dealing with the immediate response to a campus crisis. The goal of this response phase is to stabilize the scene prior to attempting resolution. Specific actions to be taken by the incident commander during a critical incident include the following:

* **Communication and Control:** Announce your command. Move the incident to a dedicated frequency if possible. Size up the situation as to "What am I dealing with?" Types of weapons, numbers of suspects, chemicals, structural problems, etc.

* **The "Hot Zone":** Early identification of the "hot zone" results in the increased safety of first responders and the general public. A portion of the initial communication to responders is to prohibit entry and movement in the hot zone and tightly control any exit from the zone.

* **Inner Perimeter:** Establish inner perimeter points to save responder and civilian lives. No unauthorized personnel are to have access to the inner perimeter. If plainclothes personnel are initially used on the inner perimeter control points, they should be replaced with uniformed personnel as soon as possible.

* **Outer Perimeter:** Establish the outer perimeter, where you are able to limit and control access into the emergency incident area. Identify safe travel routes to and from the scene. Establish media information areas.

* **The Command Post:** The incident command post should be stationed between the inner and outer perimeter. It may begin with the initial supervisors' vehicle but should transition to a good decision-making environment where commanders from the

various agencies can set up unified command using the Incident Command System (ICS).

* **The Staging Area:** Establish a staging area between the inner and outer perimeter and to position resources that will be required for resolution of the event. This is never colocated with the command post, and it may provide a backdrop for media briefings. Use of a staging area prevents gridlock and accidental entry into the hot zone.

* **Additional Resources:** Evaluate and request additional resources. This crucial step involves team assessment of the need for additional personnel, equipment, agency support or other specialized units. Early identification, requests and staging of these resources will avoid costly or dangerous delays during the incident.

Plans to effectively deal with the psychological fallout of an incident are also important. Post-incident professional counseling for personal issues requires mobilizing assistance to those who might need support. Individuals will act out differently. Quick and broad response to an incident will help lower the stress that is certain to accompany a major incident.

Instant, multi-modal communication to students and faculty during an emergency situation keeps the campus community as safe as possible. Timely warnings of significant specific crimes that threaten a campus are mandated through the Clery Act. These warnings need to include credible information that can be used to prompt immediate student and employee action in response to the event. Promulgating these warnings and informative directions to large populations on a campus remains a challenge and requires many different simultaneous signals including sirens, loudspeakers, email, text messaging, social networking tools, and word of mouth.

Building your emergency plan will identify the resources that may be needed and reasonable precautions that need to be taken against the perceived risks. However, when a major tragedy impacts a campus, the most immediate need is for a visible response that can provide reassurance that things will soon return to normal.

Taking these simple steps will pay huge dividends in the aftermath of an incident in reduced casualties, property damage, crime scene protection and the public perception of the competence of the organization's response. As the Virginia Tech tragedy demonstrated, all the time and resources devoted to resource planning are essential to an educational institution's survival. Whether the road to recovery is a quick jaunt or a marathon of a journey, the pay-off is priceless.

chapter 10

Securing Healthcare

Despite the warm-sounding name, the healthcare industry is the business of life and death. Most of the daily work in the business is mundane, procedural care of routine illnesses, preventative care, writing prescriptions, office visits, answering phone calls and responding to patient queries. For significant areas of the industry, however, life is anything but ordered and calm. Just consider the following:

At 6:30 p.m. on Saturday, June 11, 2011 onlookers observed a man they described as "disturbed" or possibly "intoxicated" entering an emergency medical facility just outside of Dayton, Ohio. Carrying a nine-milimeter handgun, this man fired a single shot that appeared to be an attempted suicide. He was taken into custody by hospital security without resistance.

And then there's the case of a physician who was shot to death on May 26, 2011 as he walked from Florida Hospital's main building to the parking garage. The shooter turned the gun on himself after killing the doctor. There's a great irony here in that the shooter was a transplant patient of the physician, whose work very likely saved his life. No clear motive has been established for the killing.

Security experts say doctors are increasingly the targets of patients' ire. "Patients do target doctors more. We see case after case of this," Russell Colling, a Colorado-based healthcare security consultant, told the Orlando Sentinel after the incident.

These cases demonstrate how easily hospitals and healthcare professionals can be vulnerable to acts of extreme and even random violence. Quoted in the *Springfield New-Sun*, Bryan Warren, President-elect of the International Association of Healthcare Safety and Security stated "Hospitals at one time were much like churches and schools, and were considered somewhat sacred. Unfortunately, that's not the case anymore. In this post-Columbine and post-Virginia Tech world, things can happen anywhere." Unfortunately, Mr. Warren is correct.

Emergency Departments Ripe for Violence

Emergency care is the epicenter of this high-intensity world of turmoil, uncertainty and risk—a place where there is open public access, and where patients of all kinds are brought in around the clock, requiring split-second decisions and treatment by medical professionals. The charged atmosphere potentially can exacerbate abusive conduct among members of medical teams, and in many emergency department (ED) situations, particularly inner-city urban locales, there is a potential for injuries resulting from gang violence, gunshot wounds and police involvement. This includes cases in which perpetrators follow the victim to the hospital to continue what started on the street.

Add to that the natural stress occurring from worry about your own health or that of a loved one, plus concerns about being underinsured to cover the sky-high costs of treatment, and you have a very volatile environment indeed.

Opportunities in healthcare for violence are not confined to the ED. One highly fertile area pertains to pharmaceuticals, particularly high street value drugs such as OxyContin. Individuals have broken into pharmacies and doctors' offices to steal these and other drugs out of desperation or for financial gain. Clearly, having such drugs is one area of high risk that requires management for healthcare professions.

What is most challenging to the healthcare industry in dealing with violence is that the profession prizes its openness and accessibility to patients and the public at large. In the face of a growing epidemic of workplace violence, healthcare must deal with the growing need to address security issues and still retain its fundamental mission to heal.

Healthcare and Violence: A Strategic View

Hospitals used to be safe havens from the violence and fear that lived on the streets. They were the place where you could be protected, find help, life, support, calm, at least. Now the game has changed and not for the better.

Hospitals, EDs and other medical facilities are faced with an ever-increasing risk of workplace violence.

As violence escalates in the healthcare workplace, established relationships, hierarchies and procedural connections between medical professionals may not allow for a real dialogue on how to deal with the threat effectively. In some cases, the situation is moving faster than people can respond to it.

Delivering healthcare is very process-driven. The system knows how to perform triage on a patient medically, but may be less successful in performing triage on the emotional and situational fallout that often comes in with the patient. The result is that some hospitals and ED units can often be more vulnerable to violent episodes than they should be.

We all would benefit from new leadership and direction in this area. By leadership, I mean a new vision of how healthcare is really working today, and some next-practices tools to help model real situations as they happen. That in turn can be the basis of new education and effective communication. The healthcare business needs to address this problem strategically from many directions, but the central and most important direction is from the heart. It has to care about its people and invest the time and effort and see this expanding threat for what it is—a danger to the growth and integrity of the healthcare industry.

The Healthcare Universe

Healthcare is an industry unlike any other, and the character of violence that it faces is similarly unique. To fully understand the critical issues, you need to look to some of the key industry authorities, in particular, the Joint Commission, an independent, not-for-profit organization that accredits and certifies more than 19,000 healthcare organizations and programs in the United States. As a certifying body, the Joint Commission gathers and maintains and encyclopedic knowledge of the healthcare industry in the United States.

The Joint Commission Report

The amount of violence at healthcare facilities has reached such a level of concern that the Joint Commission issued a Sentinel Alert in June 2010, citing assault, rape, and homicide as consistently among the top-10 serious events for which it has received reports.

Many risk factors could lead to violence in this particular workplace just because it is such a high-tension and high-traffic environment. The common factors are linked to work pressures and conflicts, emotional issues revolving around patient care, stress, personal problems, depression and financial issues. Hospital employees could experience violence in the workplace, not only from their coworkers and supervisors, but also patients and visitors.

When the extraordinary factors and complexities of delivering care are factored against the uncertainties of what a patient brings in through the door, the risks and exposure to violence may be expanded considerably. The prime directive, to save life, takes precedence while hospital staff depends upon police or security support in the event of potentially violent patients and those who have accompanied them onto the premises.

Healthcare Risk Factors: Hospital and the ED

The causes of violence at healthcare facilities are subject to changing patterns and types of crimes. The level of violence depends highly upon location and population, but these factors are not isolated to a few large cities or urban areas. They are widespread due to the prevalence of crime, the drug culture and a variety of other factors common in our society. Some of the factors identified by Occupational Safety and Health administration (OSHA) as driving risk to healthcare professionals include the following:

- **Weapons:** Access and ownership of handguns by patients, their family and friends
- **Onsite Casework:** Police casework and criminal containment at hospital sites
- **Violent Individuals:** Detainment of acutely disturbed, violent individuals at hospital sites
- **Mentally Ill Individuals:** Release of acute and mentally ill patients from hospitals without follow-up medical care
- **Drugs:** High-value drugs are available at hospitals, clinics, or pharmacy locations, which makes them likely targets for robbery
- **Open Access Waiting Areas:** Unsecured waiting rooms for clinics and hospitals where delays receiving care may lead to client volatility and hostility
- **Dangerous Individuals:** Gang members, drug or alcohol abusers or others in the waiting area or immediate treatment area who might create risk of violence

- ✦ **Reduced Staff:** Low staff levels during potential high-volume times such as mealtime, visiting time, and when staff are transporting patients
- ✦ **Isolation:** Isolated work with patients during exams or treatment
- ✦ **Remote Locations:** Solo work in remote or offsite locations with no backup or assistance
- ✦ **Lack of Education:** Lack of training in recognizing and managing escalating hostile and assaultive behavior
- ✦ **Security Failures:** Physical security failures including poorly lit parking and facility approach areas

Higher Awareness Needed

Taken together, these factors are just the tip of the iceberg. They can create a sense of collective insecurity for workers in highly exposed medical facilities that are highly at risk.

It's not enough to pretend that hospitals in high-crime areas should depend exclusively on the police or security to protect them from criminals entering their space. The level of exposure that hospital workers can face when gang members or other abusive patients and family members are present is not a simple calculus, as there isn't always an officer on hand to deal with the issues. In addition to enhanced technology to protect these venues, security also demands a high level of employee training, awareness and responsiveness, an understanding that "security is everyone's job."

 From the News: Violence on the Healthcare Frontlines

JUNE 21, 2010, PHILADELPHIA, PA. A female nurse stepped in to prevent a patient from removing needles from an empty emergency area examination room. As a result, she was attacked and beaten severely, resulting in time off at work and returning to light duty while she recuperated from her injuries. At a workplace violence event sponsored by the union, the Pennsylvania Association of Staff Nurses and Allied Professionals, the discussion focused on violence against nurses. "It's a national problem," said union president Patricia Eakin. Statistics from the U.S. Department of Labor (DOL) indicate that paramedics and nursing aides are workers most likely to miss work due to injuries. Among all workplace-related injuries violent assaults account for 38 incidents per 10,000 nurses' aides, according to a 2009 DOL study.

MARCH 17, 2011, VALLEY STREAM, NEW YORK. A nurse at local medical center was leading a group therapy session for psychiatric patients when she was attacked and injured. OSHA reviewed the case and inspected the facility. The agency determined that the facility had not put any effective workplace violence control methods into place such as violent patient screening, weapon screening, or any kind of staff training on managing workplace violence. OSHA fined the facility $4,500 for failing to protect its staff.

NOVEMBER 15, 2010, SEATTLE, WASHINGTON. Security officers working at a medical facility had registered repeated complaints over lack of appropriate equipment and security measures to protect patients and the public within the facility in the face of potentially dangerous or violent situations. The Washington Department of Labor and Industries stepped into the dispute and examined the facility and the result was a $13,200 fine concerning the failure of the facility to adequately provide tools and security to manage appropriate security. One of the key elements in the state decision to fine was failure of the facility to develop workplace violence safety programs or to properly train security officers to manage violent situations. The security officers had no training on how to appropriately manage and deal with an aggressive individual in potentially life-threatening situations. The medical facility was ordered to institute workplace violence programs to correct the situation.

Secure Healthcare through Next Practices

We're all familiar with the TV version of the operating-room drama—the tension thick as the doctor barks orders to the nurses and interns as life or death hangs in the balance. It's a cliché ingrained into our consciousness. The hero doctor and nurse, the orderlies and other characters have become standard players that unconsciously shape how we see and perceive real doctors and medical professionals in the real world.

What the TV version misses, I think, is this: For all of its new technologies and wonder drugs, the truth is that human relationships and hierarchies—the power relationships between doctors, nurses and their colleagues—remain essentially unchanged from decades ago. There is a good reason for this. In life and death situations, you need a strong and clear chain of command. There needs to be a leader who calls the shots based on knowledge and experience, particularly in urgent and time-critical situations.

That same hierarchy, however, may be blindsiding the medical community when it comes to managing workplace violence. Conventional hierarchies and organizational charts may make it difficult to share and discuss potentially difficult issues relating to internal staff bullying and abusive behavior. Under the pressure of a life-or-death emergency-care situation, some might even claim that it is acceptable for a doctor or lead caregiver to be giving orders in a rough or demanding, even abusive, fashion to subordinates. The urgency of the situation might temporarily blur the perception of acceptable behavior.

This is why I feel that next-practices thinking can have a meaningful impact in the healthcare marketplace. It's a way of enhancing the existing, proven "best practices" in order to examine the human relationships of healthcare in a fresh way. One of the most critical elements in winning the battle of workplace violence in healthcare is to open the channels of communication within the industry so that it can build new norms of behavior to handle the forces coming in from outside.

Leadership

Leadership can come from anywhere. As I've discussed, its characteristics include the sources of authoritative reference, such as the Joint Commission and OSHA, which are documenting and researching the impact of workplace violence on the healthcare industry. The key now is for healthcare organizations and their leaders to use that information to alter behavior and make new policies.

The next-practices view of leadership is that a leader can be you or a group of you, as opposed to waiting for the CEO to take some action. It's a matter of raising the flag and making people aware of what is happening and its potential consequences. Drawing upon reported events and statistical surveys is an effective way to bring credibility to your case. The authenticity of your own experience in healthcare is just as important.

You need to make people aware that situations of escalating violence that degrade the quality of healthcare also will have a broader impact than just on hospital and ED staff. They will affect a wider group of patients who expect excellent healthcare, and find that it is not available when they need it.

Education and Situation Modeling

It is ironic that in an industry with some of the most rigorous educational requirements in the world for all of its professionals—right down to the interns—there is substantially less education available for workplace violence!

In part this is understandable. Over the years, EDs have developed working rules and ad hoc solutions in coordination with local law enforcement to deal with criminal and extreme situations involving gangs and other recurring sorts of threatening problems. However, recent reports, such as those from the Joint Commission, suggest that there have been an escalation or complication of factors in the last 10 to 15 years. Acceleration of drug use, armed and dangerous shooters, money problems, gang concentrations and other factors have all played a part in accelerating the level of violence that has entered the ED and strained the ability of the institution and staff to contain the situation.

As I suggested previously, there is a demonstrated need in healthcare for a strong and centralized educational effort at all levels of the hospital and ED that teaches what I might call "situational triage." This would be the ability to read a given situation for its potential for violence and to engage law enforcement early on if necessary. It would also mean a potential recognition that hospital facilities might need some level of additional security considerations built in to accommodate situations.

From a next-practices perspective, the workplace violence continuum can function as a useful foundation document that can be used to model some specific scenarios and situations for healthcare. A strong need exists for what I call "situation modeling" that would help people visualize and see different types of healthcare-related violence and interactions played out as scenarios. It can be very difficult to absolutely define these situations, but it can be easier to show people examples of what they look like when they happen.

The point is this: The more people are educated to see, anticipate and react to potentially violent situations before they develop to a critical stage, the sooner they can access resources to head off a potentially dangerous and harmful incident.

A Violence Prevention Program for Healthcare

What are needed are clear goals and objectives to prevent healthcare workplace violence. The issue for healthcare is similar if not the same as those for any other company violence prevention program. Here are the key points I think are important:

* **Plan:** Outline a comprehensive plan for maintaining security in the healthcare workplace.

* **Commitment:** Affirm management commitment to a worker-supportive environment that places as much importance on employee safety and health as on serving the patient or client.

* **Liaison:** Establish a liaison with law enforcement representatives to prevent and mitigate workplace violence.

* **Policy:** Develop a clear policy on definition of workplace violence behaviors, with equally clear consequences for verbal and nonverbal threats and related actions. Communicate this to all managerial and staff personnel.

* **Report:** Encourage employees to promptly report incidents and suggest ways to reduce or eliminate risks.

* **Reprisal Free:** Ensure that no employee who reports or experiences workplace violence faces reprisals.

* **Responsibility:** Assign responsibility and authority for the program to individuals or teams with appropriate training and skills.

* **Briefing:** Set up a company briefing as part of the initial effort to address issues such as preserving safety, supporting affected employees and facilitating recovery.

* **Welcome:** Accept all staff suggestions and act upon those considered useful.

The critical difference to note here is the execution of the program. At each level, from the building of the plan to the management commitment, and particularly the development of a liaison with law enforcement, the focus must be on the particular character of the given healthcare institution, including its needs, location, service area, staff and other requirements.

A clearly articulated policy is particularly important because it specifies actions and consequences. This includes a zero-tolerance stance for verbal and nonverbal threats and bullying.

Above all else, it is important to remember that healthcare is a hierarchical business, particularly in the treatment hospital and ED environments, and therefore it is very important to ensure an "equality of voice" at the table for violence prevention. Everyone sees something different in the flow of people coming through the facility—from those scheduling appointments to the doctors, nurses, orderlies and technicians. Everyone's perspective counts. Prevention is a function of perspective and collaboration. The more voices and effective communication, the more effectively the organization can build a trusted dialog that can minimize and defeat workplace violence in your healthcare facility.

ROUNDTABLE
Healthcare, Women and Workplace Violence

Bill Whitmore, *Chairman & CEO, AlliedBarton Security Services*
Bonnie Michelman, *Director of Police and Outside Services, Massachusetts General Hospital*
Maureen Rush, *Vice President for Public Safety, University of Pennsylvania*
Patrick J. Wolfe, *former Vice President for Corporate Security, Cigna Corporation, retired U.S. Secret Service*

Bill Whitmore: It's both interesting and alarming that, according to OSHA, 60 percent of assaults today in the workplace happen in healthcare. Many people aren't even aware of this, but at least one healthcare company I know of has workplace violence prevention as number-one on their list.

Bonnie Michelman: It used to be that gas station and convenience store clerks were in the most dangerous professions. Now healthcare workers are in the top three or four according to the National Institute for Occupational Safety and Health.

Patrick J. Wolfe: We had a visiting nurse program for dealing with worker's compensation issues—making sure people are getting back to work—and some of that can be very dicey. Before Cigna was a healthcare company, it was also a property and casualty company, and very risk adverse. It took 19 years for the technology to catch up to what we wanted to do, but we started our current program in 1992. Getting it going in our case required constant relationships with, the ED people, who also are part of HR. Excellent people.

Whitmore: HR plays into the whole engagement factor for creating an aware employee base. So if someone comes in even from the outside and is acting a little strange, they see the warning signs early. That said, you can't just say it's only an HR issue.

Michelman: Exactly. HR isn't really involved with that patient in the hospital or that activist going after the biomedical company for doing animal testing. It is estimated that about 50 percent of all workplace violence is not employee stuff. It's outside people, including customers, patients or even random acts.

Maureen Rush: So it goes back to the regulation environment. Last time I looked at workplace violence victims, the majority are female. Is that still true?

Michelman: Actually, what is true is that the leading cause of death in the workplace for women is workplace violence, and there is a preponderance of women working in healthcare.

Rush: The newest thing in the lawsuit market in higher education is Title IX. Women are not being protected in the workplace, and I think it's just a matter of time where you are going to see a couple of Title IX lawsuits because a woman is murdered or attacked on the job.

Whitmore: But Title IX is equal treatment, equal protection.

Rush: Title IX started with the athletic areas in the universities, but it's moved into protection now. It's all about women. It's about women and equal protection. It's all about the Clery Act, which is becoming more and more complicated. It's almost like organizations need a full-time staff position just to make sure you are reporting correctly. Title IX has surfaced in civil lawsuits where rapes or murders of young woman occurred in college and university settings.

Wolfe: Ten years ago we used workplace violence language for spousal abuse threats because we felt that the value of what we were doing had to make sense to the organization. Cigna had an average of 30 to 33 percent a year of received threats to be spousal abuse cases, which we attributed to a 75 to 80 percent female employee population. The remaining were comprised of threats to our nurses who conducted visits for worker compensation cases. Our call centers also generated a large number of threats.

Michelman: In healthcare the patients are obviously stressed out. In other corporations people are losing their health benefits, causing more stress. People are just in a different place then they were years ago.

Securing Healthcare from Workplace Violence

Introducing a security program for workplace violence into any industry is complex and demanding for reasons I discuss throughout this book. Securing healthcare is to me a mix of common sense and forward thinking. It's applying next practices to how we advance the way we work with people, combined with street smarts and good old-fashioned observation to advance our physical security in the hospital and the ED. The healthcare universe demands we be smart everywhere—at the worksite and in the ways we interact with each other.

I have identified here several critical factors that I think are key from the literature provided by OSHA, the Joint Commission, and other sources that really know what's going on. These take a look at what we must to do—top of mind—to secure our healthcare universe.

Collaborative Management

What makes the program work is dialog. In healthcare this is critical—not just that the management of the healthcare facilities really gets and demonstrates that they care for the safety of their employees, but that employees get that they have to participate and work with management to make programs function from the ground up.

Managers and employees both bring their intelligence and perspectives to the table to make the program work. There is no way that an effective workplace violence solution in healthcare can be entirely "top down" or "bottom up." It has to be a family solution, with everybody seated at the table.

It's important that management be proactive about violence in the healthcare workplace. This is not some abstraction. Violence or the threat of it is happening all the time and people know it. As in any industry, leadership must be ready to build a program, stand behind it and set up standards of accountability for all employees.

Employees need to make management's commitment their own. The program won't work unless employees care about making it work. They need to understand the program and the safety and security measures. They need to attend all necessary training sessions, and report violent incidents through mandated program procedures as required. Sometimes this is cumbersome, but following the processes in a workplace violence program is how employees and managers build a culture against workplace violence. This is how new habits will get built in the ED, in the hospital wings and throughout the organization.

It's important for employees to be the program's eyes and ears. Healthcare has a very specific set of workplace violence issues, particularly in high-risk areas like the ED. The more employees observe and report incidents of violence—low-level intimidation, bullying, verbal abuse, agitation and initial assault—the more that responses and dialog about prevention can take place.

Workplace Review

A workplace review is targeted to identify vulnerabilities in the site for workplace violence. This may take the form of site design issues generally, or features of site design as they specifically relate to healthcare workflows or to the care of specific high-risk patients or care situations. Workplace analysis may include the following:

* Managing high-risk patients

* Managing patients with psychiatric or drug conditions

* Design flaws in the workplace site that create risk factors

* Isolated work areas

* Poorly lighted areas

A workplace review may include screening to review medical, safety, worker compensation and insurance records, including logs maintained by the healthcare facility and the local police to determine a history of workplace violence events at this particular facility. This level of review can be useful in determining the exposure of the facility to violence in the past and identifying future changes that need to be made to the facility's design. You can obtain detail on this type of screening from OSHA guidelines.

Risk Prevention

Risk prevention is a combination of both making physical changes to the healthcare site and management communication changes as well as how employees interact to complete business and care-delivery processes. Your workplace review may reveal specific physical site vulnerabilities, risks and hazards. Risks may be freestanding danger points in the facility design such as poorly lighted entrances or high-risk areas for patient care. They may also be elements in a workflow that need to be managed more effectively and monitored with more attention.

Hazards can be fixed in many cases by simple physical construction changes to the facility. What is important is not just slapping up random fixes but the quality of observation and thinking that goes into the adaptations to make sure that they really have the effect of enhancing employee safety and defeating workplace violence episodes. Typical examples of hazard adaptations include the following:

- **Secure service desks:** Install bullet-resistant, shatterproof glass in nurse's stations, reception, triage and admitting areas or client service rooms.
- **Safe rooms:** Create secure rooms for employees to use during a potentially violent situation.
- **Secure high-risk patient rooms:** Maintain seclusion areas for high-risk patients who might exhibit threatening or menacing behavior.
- **Secure criminal patient rooms:** Create rooms to hold and secure identified criminal patients in coordination with the police.
- **Dual exit security:** Make sure that patient care or counseling rooms have dual exits where possible to allow healthcare worker easy escape in the event of a violent incident.
- **Pathway security:** Arrange furniture to allow staff to exit easily, and secure furniture in position when possible.
- **Secure staff bathrooms:** Provide separate, secure and lockable bathrooms for staff members that are not accessible to patients.

⁇ *What's on the Minds of Today's Healthcare Security Experts?*

AlliedBarton always strives to maintain an ongoing dialog with security experts in a range of industries. It helps keep our ear to the ground in recognizing and addressing emerging concerns, and also gives us the benefit of hearing from those who deal with industry-specific issues day in and day out. It's a great forum that educates both sides. In July 2011 we held a roundtable of healthcare security experts in New York City. Here's a summary of some of their most pressing concerns. I think these are both interesting and highly useful.

What are the most significant trends or issues currently affecting security at your facility?

- Access control for open-lobby facilities.
- Inadequate resources to contain and control traffic.

- Controlling all access points to older buildings with lots of entrances.
- Maintaining a security presence with fewer resources.
- Nurses are the largest single constituency in hospital and can drive everything.

How big of an issue is workplace violence at your hospital? How do you deal with it?
- It is a big issue, especially because CMS rules on restraining patients are more restrictive.
- The three places where workplace violence is most prevalent are in-patient psych, psych emergency, and medical emergency.

What challenges do you have in addressing your top issues?
- Limited resources, can't stop everyone, lots of entry doors.
- Bringing everyone into the security program (housekeeping, doctors, nurses, etc.).
- Instilling the mindset that "security is everyone's job."

How have patient satisfaction initiatives (such as Press-Ganey/ HCAHPS) influenced your security program?
- We now provide eight hours of customer service training annually.
- Patients have expectations of security as a higher level of customer service.

How have regulations from the Joint Commission, Center for Medicare & Medicaid Services (CMS) or other regulatory bodies affected your department?
- CMS regulations are more pertinent. We can't do as much restraining, so workplace violence has increased.

What are you considering changing or improving about your security program?
- More IP cameras.
- The ability to train more than eight hours per year.
- Frequent training on "hot topics."
- Training of house medical staff is just as important to create a culture where "security is everyone's job."

Workplace Violence Victim Support

A fully developed workplace violence program should have a well-defined response process for victims after an incident has taken place. This includes psychological first aid, as well as follow-up trauma counseling, stress-debriefing and employee assistance. This is particularly important in healthcare, as employees may experience some level of workplace violence with a patient or in a critical care situation and may require immediate short-term support and care to cope with shock or to deal with the impact of the situation.

Certified professionals, psychologists, psychiatrists or social workers may provide this counseling or the healthcare facility may refer staff victims to an outside specialist. In addition, the organization may establish an employee counseling service, peer counseling or support groups.

Victims of healthcare-related workplace violence suffer a variety of consequences that may include physical or psychological injuries, such as:

* Psychological shock (short- and long-term)

* Fear of going back to the job

* Confusion as to how they are regarded by coworkers and family

* Feelings of incompetence and heightened sense of vulnerability

* Sensitivity to criticism by supervisors and managers

Having a program in place that is designed to understand this complex array of feelings can bring the impacted employee back into the fold much more quickly and effectively. You also need to engage the collective knowledge about the downstream impact of violent incident on the individual, friends and coworkers and the institution itself. Not doing so serves only to perpetuate the violence through ignorance or inattention.

Victim support is also a vital element in the overall learning effort about workplace violence that is at the heart of the culture-building process. The more you understand the recovery process from individual incidents of workplace violence, the better you can manage the whole process effectively, and the better you can protect people from the negative consequences and the harm this generates. We know the pain that the attack or assault can cause, and we know that the aftermath is often an isolation of the victim in fear and insecurity. By helping victims through these periods, you will build a stronger program for everybody.

Safety and Health Training

In my experience, people always tend to resist the idea of taking safety training, but they are glad they participated once it's over. Workplace violence programs depend on effective training. There is a core concept—"universal precautions for violence"—at the heart of workplace violence training. To me it means that the more you train, the more prepared you are to handle the unknown, the unexpected and the random violence that may occur. Nowhere is this more important than in healthcare.

The core of all safety and health training is modeling key situations that may take place around violent events. There are no clean absolutes to these situations, even allowing that there are some similar populations and recurring factors. Training must make individuals alert to the fact that healthcare workplace violence events may take a variety of forms and will emerge from any number of situations. Training will be more effective if it is built around good models and scenarios, and helps people see the key risk factors and sharpens their observational skills.

Safety and health training for workplace violence may cover a wide range of topics, depending upon the needs of the healthcare facility, the scope of treatment offered and the patient clientele. In all cases, however, the training should represent a mix of the structure of the workplace violence program and include functional elements to teach employees how to recognize violent situations, how to manage them and how to work together and collaborate on minimizing their impact. Typical components of safety and health training include the following:

- **Policy Details:** The organization's or facility's workplace violence policy
- **Risk Factors:** Key risk factors that cause or contribute to assaults
- **Warning Signs:** Modeling and scenarios of escalating behavior of warning signs that may lead to assaults
- **Diffuse Situations:** Methods to prevent or diffuse volatile situations or aggressive behavior
- **Anger Management:** Techniques to manage anger and appropriately use medications as chemical restraints
- **Action Plan:** Standard response action plan for violent situations including alarms, assistance and communications in place

- ✦ **Control Methods:** Progressive behavior control methods including safe methods to apply restraints
- ✦ **Safety Devices:** The location and operation of safety devices such as alarm systems, along with the required maintenance schedules and procedures.
- ✦ **Buddy System:** Collaborative methods to protect one's self and coworkers

The functional reality of safety and health training is a deeper awareness. The purpose is to communicate strength and clarity without transmitting fear. The more people can see through these behaviors of patients and high-risk individuals, and have a clear response path to them, the more they will have clear ownership of their own safety and be ready to take charge in difficult situations.

Secure Health

Healthcare is a dramatically growing world of workplace violence. Why? It may be that we depend on the healthcare business for much more in our lives, and it may be simply that our culture has grown more violent and dependent on drugs, and these factors are coming back to haunt us.

Whatever the causes and the contributing factors, the challenges are escalating dramatically, putting healthcare workers at risk. There is a strong need to build new dialogs within the time-honored healthcare culture and hierarchies to allow all parties to collaborate on workplace violence policies, particularly in the high-tension environment of the ED.

A formula for success will involve both reorienting how people communicate and observe potential areas of risk, and understanding how those observations translate to changes to the worksite and facilities. Healthcare workers are just now beginning to face their own vulnerabilities, and it is essential that they create a safe work environment so they can function and grow professionally.

GUEST EXPERT
Creating a Safer Emergency Department

By Ken Bukowski, *Vice President, Healthcare, AlliedBarton Security Services*

When I talk with hospital administrators, the fear of violence in their emergency departments is always a concern. With EDs across the country experiencing longer wait times and seeing more disgruntled patients, it's no wonder hospitals are reporting an increase in violent behavior.

According to the Emergency Nurses Association, one in four ED nurses has been physically assaulted more than 20 times in the past three years. The Federal Substance Abuse and Mental Health Services Administration recently reported a 24-percent increase in violent acts in EDs caused by patients who were brought in because of a drug- or alcohol-related incident, and in 2010 the Joint Commission issued a sentinel alert. These types of reports are enough to keep any hospital administrator up at night.

Healthcare facilities and especially emergency departments present unique security challenges. However, you can take steps to further protect your ED and the entire healthcare facility. The following tips can help keep your patients and staff safe:

+ Conduct a thorough security assessment to identify areas that need improved lighting, surveillance and overall safety. Pay close attention to all points of entry.

+ Encourage staff to report any sign of violent behavior and develop a reporting system so they know when and how to report their concerns. Every complaint should be taken seriously.

+ Train staff to recognize the signs of potential violent behavior such as loud conversation, anxious or aggressive behavior, abusive language and hostile facial expressions or gestures.

+ Consider upgrading or installing additional closed-circuit TV cameras throughout the hospital to include critical systems, sensitive areas and loading docks.

+ Hire security officers that are specially trained in healthcare and understand and respect the hospital culture and setting.

Special training for the ED staff is vital so they can learn to recognize abnormal behavior and know how to diffuse a violent situation. Your staff needs to be confident in the plan and understand the major role they play in keeping the ED safe. Make sure that your staff understands that violence against them is never appropriate and that someone is available for them to contact.

Security should be available to staff at all times to make sure they are comfortable in all situations with patients. Security officers are trained to deescalate difficult situations and can be a great resource for your ED staff. Inquire about what extra services your security program can provide to increase safety, such as walking escorts.

It is important to remember that plans must be shared and implemented to be effective and no plan is complete without continued review and drills. Staff will feel more comfortable knowing that they have completed drills and will be more confident if a situation does occur.

chapter 11

Looking Ahead to a Secure, Successful Future

I titled this book *Potential*, and of course I intended that to have a double meaning—one that should be pretty obvious by now. As a leader your commitment to act on the potential for workplace violence will help your organization achieve its full potential—not only making it safer, but in helping it operate more efficiently, achieving better success at fulfilling its goals whether they are commercial or otherwise.

As I've stated throughout the book, this is a matter of building a successful culture where employees feel safe, not threatened, and not maligned by their bosses. It's a culture where employees understand the range and varieties of workplace violence and its warning signs, and feel empowered to do something about it. It's a culture with a zero-tolerance policy for any inappropriate or troubling behaviors that could lead to a tragic incident and that themselves are lower forms of violence.

Potential is everywhere, both good and bad, and that pretty well sums up the way I look at workplace violence and the value of building a strong organizational culture to combat it. In this final chapter I touch on some of the issues that have formed the core of this book, with a perspective on the workplace security challenges and opportunities that face all of us going forward.

Trends in Workplace Violence, Today and Tomorrow

I live outside of Philadelphia. Recently there were flash mob problems occurring in the city—marauding individuals were beating people up, robbing them. As I write this, the same thing has been going on in London, of all places—senseless rioting and looting that has continued for days. Something is going on in society right now that is very troubling to me, and that has been spilling over into the workplace.

Deaths from violent incidents have actually declined for more than a decade, according to the U.S. Department of Labor, which found that the number of workplace homicides had fallen from a high of 1,080 in 1994 to 526 in 2008, a decline of 51 percent. Much of this is attributed to increased awareness, training and early intervention in the workplace, as well as improved security in businesses such as convenience stores and other retail establishments. Another reason is ever more timely and effective medical intervention. Medical personnel now triage people more quickly, and as a result of that you may not have as many deaths.

However, despite the drop in workplace homicides, it appears that overall incidents—verbal abuse, harassment, and lesser forms of intimidation—are as persistent as ever. An estimated 43,800 acts of harassment, bullying, and other threatening behavior occur in the workplace every day. According to the most recent large national survey on workplace bullying, 37 percent of the U.S. workforce (an estimated 54 million Americans) reports being bullied at work; an additional 12 percent witness it, according to the Bureau of Labor Statistics.

The environment for people acting out is ripe right now because of the economy—joblessness and an increased sense of hopelessness for many. It also may stem from the political battles going on in Washington and elsewhere, exacerbated by the 24-hour news cycle that constantly bombards us with bad news and violent outbursts around the world.

I was talking with some young people recently about the workplace violence issue and it was interesting what they said. "Do you understand how many people of our age are upset?" they asked me. "We did everything right, we did everything that we were told to do and we are stuck. We can't find jobs, we're stuck living with our parents or brothers and sisters, and there are a lot of people who are upset out there about this."

Certainly, in these unstable times there is higher risk for stress, isolation, hopelessness and everyday pressures and troubles that can lead to violence in the workplace. There also seems to be shorter hair-trigger responses and less resistance to advocating and perpetrating violence for a strongly held belief or cause—ranging from rigid, fundamentalist religious dogma to passionately held views about the treatment of animals, children, ethnic groups, political causes—you name it. These are among the top trends in workplace violence today and tomorrow, requiring even more vigilance among all engaged leaders and employees.

The Largest Workplace Violence Issue

Given the reality of the types of workplace violence we've heard about way too often in the past, coupled with the emerging trends of tomorrow, what is the single largest workplace violence issue that organizations face today? I'd say it is simply a lack of awareness.

Almost every workplace violence issue you hear about is one where "no one saw it coming" and that is often attributable to a lack of awareness. In 95 percent of the cases you can be sure that, after the fact, once you're looking in the proverbial rearview mirror, it becomes painfully obvious that someone should indeed have seen it coming. All the signs were there, with the perpetrator feeling disrespected, distant, disconnected. Perhaps the person had been acting strangely, sullen, depressed or withdrawn, with unexplained increase in absenteeism, changes in appearance and hygiene, or has been exhibiting an increased use of drugs or alcohol, or comments about weapons or suicide and so on.

These are the issues that all people in every organization need to be attuned to, because it's dangerously lacking now. And, if you're in a business with a high level of public interaction—healthcare, government, education and retail—your risk is going to be higher still, making your educated awareness even more of a necessity.

Of course, there's no guarantee. There always are the "outliers"—that relatively small subset of individuals who commit a terribly violent act with no prior warning whatsoever. And even when the signs are there, it's not always easy to detect them while navigating all of the other challenges such as privacy concerns, HIPPA, employment laws, and so forth. The sad truth is that there is no way to prevent every single workplace violence incident. However, there is no doubt that an effective approach to prevention is to create a culture like the one I suggest in this book— one in which the participants are able to recognize, report and respond to the potential of violence with the organization's full support.

In the face of workplace violence you can harden your assets so that your people and property are at less risk. However, that has to be coupled with constantly pressing a culture where participants are aware of the warning signs, and inappropriate behavior of any kind simply isn't acceptable.

Acting on the Continuum

Understanding and acting on potential workplace violence—and I'm talking about the whole continuum of behaviors—will help an organization build that critical awareness it needs to achieve its full potential. You have to understand it, and you have to act on it, because if you don't those behaviors flourish and your organization is simply not going to be a very good one. If you have caring, understanding and helpfulness, you don't have a culture of bullies and others who may want to act on their frustrations and despair.

You hear about organizations that are not very nice places to work. Years ago, conversations about the Postal Service often tended to carry the common themes that management didn't care, yet nobody talked about it. Well, you know what happened there. Unfortunately, the term "going postal" has become synonymous with the most tragic kind of workplace violence.

The Case for National Background Screening

Among the tools that would help us in facing the workplace violence prevention challenges of today and tomorrow is enhanced screening on a national level. However, implementing a comprehensive system that all organizations can use is fraught with complexity and conflicting issues related to state legislation and social trends.

Background screening is a tool and practice we use a lot in the private security industry, with lessons that may be helpful when looking at the larger picture for all organizations. Where I reside and work in southeastern Pennsylvania, the state law governing private security companies was written in 1952, the year I was born. It has never been changed despite the fact that we now have a national and even global economy where everyone is interconnected more than ever before.

In this day and age many organizations operate on a national and even global level, recruiting from a talent pool that also transcends political borders, yet screening databases rarely talk to each other state to state. You can do a criminal record check and in your county that comes up clean, even when the same person may have committed ten crimes three counties away. You have to use multiple databases. For example, a national fingerprint database called IDENT theoretically will tell you whether an individual has even been arrested or gone into a prison system in America. There's still work to be done, but these systems are getting better all the time.

There is also a national record deposit that the FBI runs out of West Virginia called Integrated Automated Fingerprint Identification System (IAFIS) that law enforcement taps into—but this database and IDENT are both incomplete, with many thousands of old-style nondigital fingerprints yet to be entered.

Still, these databases could be incredibly useful if our industry—and any business, really—could be permitted through federal legislation to tap into them. With one stroke, using digital fingerprints, you could run a national search on someone. If an individual had a criminal record in any state you would find out about it.

However, the reality is that national searches are not available to most organizations. The processes from state to state are similar, but they're all separate with no interoperability. Background checks and the laws that enable such queries are not nationally driven, leaving huge gaps in what could be critical information about a new hire. A number of commercial outfits will run some kind of check for you that extends beyond just your state, but they're not necessarily comprehensive.

Certain segments of the business world are allowed access to true national databases—for example, bank tellers, casino workers and others. So, that kind of information is available—just not to most companies. The private security industry has been working to promote federal legislation that would permit private companies such as ours access to that national database, but it is an uphill battle. Currently there are 16 states in this country that don't even have laws regulating private security companies. Others have laws that regulate the industry, but do not provide for access to the national databases.

So what we are looking for in my industry is not to circumvent the state system. We simply believe that each of our companies should be state-regulated as a business, but at the same time have access to the national database. The same could be said of any organization looking to assure that its new hires have no serious background issues that could portend trouble in the days ahead.

Screening Is a Filter, Not a Solution

Ultimately, background screening—whether national or statewide—is a useful filter and tool to help you make an evaluation during the hiring process. It's not a guarantee that the person you hire will never commit an act of workplace violence. If you do a background check and think that it is going to get you off the hook for any problems going forward, well, that's just not the case. Still, it is useful, and will be most valuable when used as part of a comprehensive workplace violence prevention program built upon the principles I've put in this book.

ROUNDTABLE
Making Workplace Violence Prevention a Core Strategy

Bill Whitmore, *Chairman & CEO, AlliedBarton Security Services*
Rich Cordivari, *Vice President, National Accounts, AlliedBarton Security Services*
Bonnie Michelman, *Director of Police and Outside Services, Massachusetts General Hospital*
Maureen Rush, *Vice President for Public Safety, University of Pennsylvania*
Chris Swecker, *former Assistant Director Criminal Investigative Division, FBI*
Patrick J. Wolfe, *former Vice President for Corporate Security, Cigna Corporation, retired U.S. Secret Service*

Bill Whitmore: Part of our thesis in this book is that workplace violence and its prevention is a critical concern for every organization, and should be for every leader. Engaged leaders don't produce an environment where there is bullying and intimidation going on. They don't tolerate it. So how do we change what appears to be the prevailing mentality of not considering this a front-burner item?

Maureen Rush: The organizations that have changed that mentality and now have workplace violence prevention plans in place are often the ones who suffered some major crisis. I talk to colleagues in the university market who think they are safe, but weird things happen in "safe" environments. Until people have that scare, they are not going to embrace the idea of talking about it.

Rich Cordivari: Also, there may be a crisis management plan and it's assumed that something about workplace violence is in there, so when a crisis comes you have to dust it off. However, the plan may include only fire, and if there's anything at all about workplace violence, the focus is on response once something happens. It's not a prevention protocol.

Whitmore: You have to have a safety atmosphere, a workplace attitude that safety is important. If you see something say something. Unfortunately, a lot of companies think that they don't have time for that, because they are so focused on trying to survive in this economy.

Chris Swecker: Right after the Virginia Tech incident a North Carolina college blue-ribbon panel came together, studied the issue and made recommendations. I think an awareness level exists in the university system, but at the corporate level there needs to be an awakening of some kind or a different mindset.

Rush: My sales pitch to people above my pay scale is that there is a reputational risk for the university should any kind of serious event occur. Maybe universities are a little ahead of that curve because parents are paying $50,000 to $60,000 a year for their kids. I don't know any organization that does not have a crisis management plan, but workplace violence prevention should be folded into that plan.

A Tough Challenge: Employing Ex-Cons

Unfortunately, I don't see the political will to make a national background screening database happen anytime soon. I'd love to see it made available to all organizations, but the reality of it is there are numerous initiatives in the country right now that are focused in almost the opposite direction— getting those who have served time for crimes back to work.

I recently went to a presentation by Philadelphia Mayor Michael J. Nutter, who said that if we are going to improve the situation for these folks, then somebody has to take a chance and employ them. I absolutely understand that and support the mayor's initiative. But I also believe that such a decision depends on a rather subjective evaluation. Many people at some point in their life have made serious legal mistakes, with no indication of violence then, or maybe in the years or decades since. But you have others whose rap sheets are covered with violent behavior. Consequently, this is the sort of thing that needs to be evaluated on a case by case basis.

The Festering Issue of True Believers

As I discuss earlier in the book, true believers are people who are so obsessed and passionate about their cause that they feel anything is justifiable in defense of their beliefs. Although this category of workplace violence threat has been around for decades, it seems to me to be an area that requires an ever more vigilant focus going forward.

As illustrated by the attempted airline terrorist "underwear bomber" attack on Christmas 2009, where a man tried to detonate explosives in his clothes while onboard Northwest Airlines flight 253 from Amsterdam to

Detroit, our country continues to be a target for these kinds of terrorists. They can range from foreign nationals like that person and the 9/11 and U.S. Cole bombers, to domestic terrorists such as Timothy McVey, or Nidal Malik Hasan, who opened fire and killed 14 people, wounding 29 at Fort Hood in November 2009. (A subsequent plot against Fort Hood by an entirely different person was thwarted in the summer of 2011.) They also can be animal rights activists, radical abortion opponents set on bombing clinics, and so on.

The Role of Security Officers

As a nation that has lived through the horrors of 9/11 and Hurricane Katrina, coupled with ongoing Homeland Security warnings and efforts to support those suffering from disasters elsewhere, such as Haiti or Japan, we understand that emergency preparedness is crucial to our mutual security. Whether natural or man-made, emergencies can wreak havoc and result in losses of lives and property. However, not all emergencies become disasters —the difference is in how effectively people respond.

Today's emergency preparedness and response training is far more advanced than in years past. Bioterrorism and anthrax have become household words, and all people need to be properly trained to respond to a variety of situations, and security officers are a key part of the prevention stance. With the proper training, security officers can secure a dangerous area, evacuate buildings and coordinate emergency response. Additionally, security officers play a key role in preventing emergencies by monitoring building access, conducting patrols and ensuring that safety and security procedures are followed. But before any of these activities can occur, the proper training, specific to the officer's site, is needed.

Expanded emergency training for security officers has led to improved relationships with law enforcement, government agencies and the general public. Of course, security officers and law enforcement personnel aren't the only individuals who can benefit from emergency preparedness training. Civilians can take a proactive approach to emergency preparedness so they too can take an active role during an emergency. Readily available automatic external defibrillators and a general public that is well-versed in such equipment and accustomed to seeing it in public is just one example of our nation's acceptance of the individual's role in emergency response. A prepared individual is better equipped to evacuate, help others and do whatever is needed in an emergency.

When the next emergency occurs, security, law enforcement and prepared citizens can work together for the good of everyone.

Hiring Military Veterans

I don't want to complete this book without including a word about hiring military veterans. If your company's diversity recruiting strategy fails to include military veterans, you are missing out on working with some of our country's most outstanding men and women. Organizations that fail to recognize the extraordinary leadership qualities that veterans bring to the workplace pass up the opportunity to work with results-oriented employees that have a strong sense of accountability and responsibility—all attributes that will benefit your workplace violence prevention program and your organization as a whole. It is time for our country's corporate leaders to awaken to the reality that combat leadership and military discipline translate into dynamic employees who can enhance an organization's productivity and safety.

While the national unemployment rate hovers over nine percent for civilians, the unemployment rate for young male veterans, including those returning from Afghanistan and Iraq, is more than double the national average, at 21.6 percent, according to the Bureau of Labor Statistics. Isn't it time to shine the employment spotlight on the brave men and women who serve our country?

What essential life skills do military veterans bring to foreword-thinking organizations that make for an indispensable pairing? The military trains our men and women to lead by example, as well as to understand the nuances of delegation and motivation. As General Douglas McArthur once said, "A true leader has the confidence to stand alone, the courage to make tough decisions, and the compassion to listen to the needs of others."

Military veterans understand the value of teamwork, which they can apply in our country's offices and boardrooms. Veterans understand their role within an organizational framework and serve as exemplary role models to subordinates while demonstrating accountability, leadership and growth to supervisors.

Veterans generally enter the workforce with identifiable skills that can be transferred to the business world and are often skilled in technical trends pertinent to business and industry. And what they don't know, they are eager to learn, making them receptive and ready hires in work environments that value ongoing learning and training. Veterans represent diversity and collaborative teamwork in action, having served with people from diverse economic, ethnic and geographic backgrounds. Even under dire stress, veterans complete tasks and assignments in a timely manner as they have labored under restrictive schedules and resources on the battlefields and in the military installations where they've served.

Employers can find qualified veterans from a variety of sources, including the Employer Partnership of the Armed Forces, Employer Support of the Guard and Reserve, Military.com, HireVeterans.com, and the Wounded Warriors Project. As an employer, you can become true partners with selected veterans' organizations and work with them proactively to ensure that you are maximizing your ability to recruit from this extremely qualified talent pool.

Lest we forget, the men and women who have chosen to serve our country are patriots who have made enormous sacrifices to ensure our safety and freedom. By employing military veterans, we are saying "thank you for your service" and expressing gratitude for protecting us from terrorism and other threats.

Full Potential through Leadership

I know that I've been harping on leadership again and again in this book, and for good reason. Understanding workplace violence, establishing next practices, engaging employees, providing for their personal and professional development, making sure they understand their role in helping to prevent incidents—that's all essential stuff. But the glue that holds it all together is leadership. And that's why I wrote this book, aimed at leaders like you.

Effective workplace violence prevention doesn't happen by itself. It's a matter of leadership setting a culture. Unless you address this, unless you talk about having a culture that doesn't accept being bullied, then no one will be capable of reaching that level. So I'll say it again: As an organizational leader, you need to create the environment that helps prevent workplace violence from happening.

You can extend this concept and say that employees need to feel safe and secure and therefore be enabled to feel good about recognizing and reporting unusual behavior. This is important, because saying something may go against their conditioning. If leadership in an organization creates a culture where the good kind of preventive behavior is actually encouraged, where employees understand they have the organization's support—if they see something to say something—that can make a big difference.

My staff and I were talking in a leadership meeting recently about Maslow's hierarchy of needs, and how people must feel safe and secure in their environment so they can perform better. When you give people the pathway and the means to improve themselves, both professionally and personally, they can reach their full potential, and so can your organization.

You can take this matter one step further and say that employees have to feel safe in their ability and obligation to report issues when they see something odd. They also have to feel safe in their day-to-day lives. If somebody is going to work every day thinking "Am I going to be harassed, am I going to be beat up, am I going to be vilified for somebody else's mistakes?" then they are never going to reach their full potential.

So leadership influences are critical, including your management skills and the culture that encourages and educates people to employ an effective management aesthetic. There could be many cases where people aren't the most highly skilled managers, and rather than encouraging people to grow and do good they intimidate them, which not only suppresses their ability to do tasks well but can also anger them—so that's part of the problem too.

The Cutting Edge of Workplace Violence Prevention

Ultimately, what would I identify as the cutting edge of workplace violence prevention? I think it's that it has become part of the conversation. If anything is cutting edge it's the fact that people are talking about it, and trying to figure out next practices for dealing with the reality.

Look at all the discussions we are having about it. You are now seeing leaders looking strategically at workplace violence prevention, and recognizing that having an environment free of these issues is good for the organization.

The two concepts go hand in hand. Typically you train your communications people who are going to be laying this out and talking about it to others. This is what AlliedBarton's Vice President, National Accounts Rich Cordivari, until recently our Vice President of Learning and Development, has been doing for our workplace violence prevention awareness at our company and among our customers.

It happens all the time: Companies are coming to us and saying "we really want to take a stance here," recognizing that any of the behaviors on our workplace violence continuum are not acceptable at their places of business.

Doing something about workplace violence means drawing up a tactical plan that includes everyone in the company and is reflected in your core document. A lot of tactics go into such an effort, as described throughout this book, but your plan—your written policy—is the baseline reference.

Take our own company as an example. Our *Dare to be GREAT* value statement includes our leadership non-negotiables. We are saying to each new employee, "Here's your booklet, here's our culture and here's what we expect from you as a leader." And when you read those leadership non-negotiables, you see that they're all about building a culture opposite one that would have a lot of the behaviors of workplace violence.

Your policy as reflected in your own value statement must include every employee, from leadership to midlevel managers, from administrative workers to security personnel to HR. It needs to enable individuals to step up and say this type of behavior is not acceptable. They need to pick up the phone or send an email. Training helps everyone know what to do. It's a conversation we all have to continue.

Measuring Progress

How can you measure your progress in building effective workplace violence prevention? One way you can do it is to set program goals—a reduction of incidents at all levels. You begin by setting benchmarks today and work from there. Let's say you conduct a survey in your organization that asks "In your daily work routines are you intimidated, bullied or subject to discrimination?" You measure responses to this question, and then implement a workplace violence awareness and prevention program using the guidance in this book. A year after the outset of the program you conduct the survey again, then again at two years, and so on. That should provide you with some effective measurement of the success of your program.

Three Takeaways

When people ask me why I decided to write this book, I give a lot of reasons but the most fundamental reason is that I read the data that reveals that security practitioners regard violence as their number-one concern in the workplace. Combine that with the fact that 70 percent of organizations have no formal workplace violence prevention policy, and you can probably see my motivation. If this book raises awareness of workplace violence prevention and leaves you with a deeper understanding of the three takeaways that follow, then I will consider this project to have been well worth my time.

Takeaway #1: Heed the Wakeup Call
The first takeaway is that this book should be a wake-up call. If you didn't believe before that workplace violence is a critical issue for any organization, including yours, then I hope you will now.

Takeaway #2: Believe the Experts
The second takeaway that I'd like for you to get from this book is that you as an organizational leader need to put workplace violence on the table as part of your strategic planning. You may previously have been not paying attention to this issue, or perhaps you did not understand it, but you as a leader have got to take action when you are planning for your company. When you are putting all of your organization's issues on the table, and your chief security officer or somebody similar with a c-suite title is telling you that they have a real concern about workplace violence, then workplace violence prevention has got to be part of your overall strategic plan.

Takeaway #3: Workplace Violence Is a Continuum
The third takeaway, and the highlight of the book for me, is the idea that workplace violence typically occurs on a continuum. It starts small and then it gets big. You rarely see an incident that starts out at the top of the scale. It's frequently a progression, which means that in many cases it can be recognized and stopped early—which is good news.

Part of this issue is understanding that behavior matching any level of the continuum is going to prevent you from getting the full potential of your employees. The lower forms of workplace violence are disruptive to productivity and bad for morale. Nobody wants to work for or with anyone who disrespects them, speaks poorly to them and generally doesn't give them the time of day. These are all forms of harassment, and you need to get a handle on them throughout your organization. With a disrespectful, aimless culture, you will get an employee that says "forget this guy; I'm going to do what I want to do. I'm going to put out the least I can." Such a person may

Workplace Violence Continuum

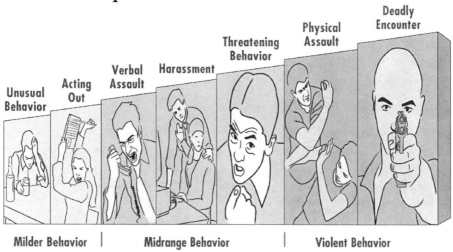

Good leadership impacts every step of the workplace violence continuum.

decide to retaliate, sabotage, do work incorrectly or go up the continuum of violent behavior. It's a lit fuse.

Reach Your Potential

I often present keynotes on how to drive business performance through leadership branding. As you've read in these pages, we do this at AlliedBarton by putting in place leaders and employee engagement programs that drive performance, thereby nurturing and delivering professionals who enhance our brand through their behavior. Our executives and security officers alike are always expected to lead by example, promote and embody the culture, values and benefits of the company, and to do so with passion and ownership.

Workplace violence prevention flows from and is a key benefit of this same system. Our leadership performance branding efforts and our workplace violence prevention program essentially are one and the same.

How do you distinguish value in your own organization, and how does that impact your business results? We have found that strong leadership increases employee attitude, customer service and bottom-line profitability. Our operational non-negotiables are a huge part of this – a strategic essential to both the safety and success of our company that also leads to enhanced growth, quality control and assurance.

When your organization takes good care of its brand by creating leaders and establishing strong safety cultures based on respect and accountability, you empower your employees to be competitive. Doing so allows them to continue to be relevant, challenged, engaged and productive—not only in the service of your business goals, but in proactively participating in keeping the organization safe and secure.

AlliedBarton began as a small company and today we are the largest American-owned security services provider, thanks to the dedication of our employees. And while we have grown and changed, our focus on leadership, employee advancement and career development has not. Creating and nurturing a comprehensive, nurturing culture at AlliedBarton ensures that we are developing leaders who are committed to fulfilling our core mission while keeping our company safer. That's a philosophy that can apply to all of us. By addressing potential on all levels, you will reach it.

appendix

Workplace Violence Awareness and Prevention Resources

Potential: Workplace Violence Prevention and Your Organizational Success
http://www.potentialthebook.com/

AlliedBarton's Workplace Violence Resources
http://www.alliedbarton.com/SecurityResourceCenter/WorkplaceViolence.aspx

Occupational Safety and Health Administration
This Workplace Violence website provides information on the extent of violence in the workplace, assessing the hazards in different settings and developing workplace violence prevention plans for individual worksites.
http://www.osha.gov/SLTC/workplaceviolence/index.html

NIOSH—Occupational Violence
The National Institute for Occupational Safety and Health's website offers research on occupational violence and homicide.
http://www.cdc.gov/niosh/topics/violence/

Violence in the Workplace—The Role of the Facility Manager
This report, sponsored by the IFMA Foundation, looks at the history of workplace violence, provides operational definitions, examines the current scope of the problem, discusses regulations and statutes and, provides tools for planning, responding and recovering from WPV.
http://www.ifmafoundation.org/files/WorkplaceViolence.pdf

The USDA Handbook of Workplace Violence Prevention and Response
The USDA offers an overview of workplace violence, including prevention, identification, response and resources to learn more.
http://www.usda.gov/news/pubs/violence/wpv.htm

Index

deadly encounters, 11, 17, 200

decision making, ethical, 20, 110, 150

denial, 32–35, 42, 44

Department of Homeland Security, vii, xviii, 175

discipline, 14–15

doctors, 179

documentation, 165–166, 187

Domenico, David, 4–5

domestic violence, 8

"Door Opener" communication, 117

Dorn, Randy, 113

drug-induced violence, 13, 55, 180, 182

drug testing, 162

dual exit security, 192

E

e-learning, 133

Eakin, Patricia, 183–184

EAP. see employee assistance program

education, 105, 183, 186

   AlliedBarton EDGE®, 126

   awareness, 139–142

   e-learning, 133

   for employees, 138–139

education sector, 52–53

   campus violence, 56–57, 204–205

   crisis planning for college campuses, 174–177

   risk analysis for, 52, 67

email, 88

emergencies, behavioral, 145

emergency departments (EDs), 180, 190, 197–198

   risk factors for violence in, 182–183

   tips to help keep patients and staff safe, 197

violence in, 55, 182–183, 197

emergency medical facilities, 179

emergency plans, 142, 176

emergency room assaults, 54, 55

emotional damage, long-term, 46–47

employee assistance program (EAP), 140–141, 144, 147–148

employee awareness, 111–112, 139–142

employee engagement, 84, 97, 105, 111–112, 115–116, 116–118

   AlliedBarton EDGE® program, 126

   culture of, 106, 109–111, 112

   examples of, 108

   next practices, 69, 72

   nurturing, 20, 92, 105–118

   tools for, 110

employee evaluation, 101, 129–130

employee handbooks, 22

employee morale, 84

employee pay, 84, 111

"employee shooter" scenario, 49

employees, xvii

   attitudes and actions for creating security, 97

   background screening, 70, 162, 167–168, 202–204

   educating, 138–139

   empowerment of, 91, 105, 139

   engaged, 20

   ex-cons, 205

   as most valuable resources, 116–118

   next practices for, 72

   non-negotiables for, 110–111

   recognition of, 98, 108, 114

   relations with, 111

   response to incidents, 144–145

   support for, 38, 89

CPSIA information can be obtained at www.ICGtesting.com
Printed in the USA
LVOW082331270112

265973LV00001B/6/P